TEN MARATHONS

SEARCHING FOR THE SOFT GROUND IN A HARD WORLD

DOUG SCHNEIDER

D0109091

SAYBROOK PUBLISHING

TEN MARATHONS

Searching for the Soft Ground in a Hard World

Doug Schneider

PRAISE FOR TEN MARATHONS ...

Reading Doug Schneider's insightful *Ten Marathons*, I felt as if I had discovered a long-lost sibling or alter ego. He runs and thinks and appreciates life in ways that resonate deeply. This has nothing to do with running the Boston Marathon or crushing your personal best. It has everything to do with opening your eyes wide, breathing deeply, and following the trail around the next bend. Schneider writes that running makes him "feel totally alive and in the moment." That's how I felt as I savored *Ten Marathons*. It reminded me of all I love about reading and running.

Amby Burfoot, winner 1968 Boston Marathon; author, Run Forever

www.AmbyBurfoot.com (for books and personal info)

As much a meditation on life as it is on running, Doug Schneider's memoir *Ten Marathons* is a beautifully-written ode to the activity that irrevocably changed him in more ways than just physical.

Bestselling memoirist Rachael Herron

Ten Marathons is a fun read. I relate to Doug Schneider's obsession with running. Having found running as the only sport I am good at, I have now been running for over 65 years. During that time, I have in over 300 cities and towns and 15 countries. We runners have found running to be part of our 'being.'

Kent Friel, legendary Cincinnati distance runner, 58-time-finisher of Cincinnati Thanksgiving Day Race

Ten Marathons is a fantastic book for those who love a great life story told in a humorous, yet insightful manner. This book will not only make you feel happy but will help you understand how success depends on facing adversity and then overcoming it. It will entertain and motivate. Whether you're a marathoner or a couch potato, you will be deeply moved by *Ten Marathons*. Doug is not only a successful executive, entrepreneur and roadrunner, he is also a philosopher who understands what it takes to live successfully in today's complicated world.

Robert Pasick PhD, Psychologist and Executive Coach, Founder of Leaders Connect

The philosopher Schopenhauer said, "Men spend their lives either reflecting on the past or anticipating the future, so therefore they miss the moment, living in the state of in between."

James Joyce, in his mighty classic novel Ulysses, said, "As a philosopher he knew that at the termination of any allotted life only an infinitesimal part of a person's desires has been realized."

And Hemingway answered, when asked, 'Why do you write? Are you kidding? Cause some day I am going to be dead."

Doug Schneider's philosophical contemplative assessment of the age-old question, "Why do we run?" gets answered in his book *Ten Marathons,* with, "Now is Now, its later than you think, cause some day I am going to be .... So, we run on, people against the current, marching to whatever we want it to be."

Dr. Stacy Osborne, Podiatrist, author of "A Normal Life Synchronicity Changed," (Read it free on line at www.flipreality.net)

PROLOGUE

M *arch 2018, Hilton Head, South Carolina*

"The idea of suffering is so natural to both writers and runners it seems to be a common bond. And therefore no surprise when one turns out to be both."
Dr. George Sheehan, Running & Being: The Total Experience

I CALL Mom on Sunday afternoon, as I always do. She sounds groggy and awful. Maybe she just woke up, even though it is two in the afternoon. Or maybe her condition has begun to affect her ability to speak clearly, I can't tell. She has inoperable oral cancer with a terminal diagnosis. A few months ago, I got a call from the surgeon at Ohio State. Like most surgeons, he was willing to operate (again), but when I asked if he would do so on his own eighty-seven-year-old mother with dementia, he was clear that he would not. Chemo and radiation are hard enough to withstand without the fact that your memory is also fading rapidly. My sister Susan, who, to her everlasting credit, is my mom's primary caretaker, explains to me that Mom has just woken up. She probably just needs some food and she will be better.

Fifteen minutes after I hang up the phone, Susan calls back. Mom isn't any better. She has gone back to bed without eating anything. Not surprisingly for someone in her mental and physical state, Mom is having not just good days and bad days but good moments and bad moments. This is a bad moment, if not a bad day, if not the beginning of the end. Susan sounds scared, which is unusual since—while she is doing a great job of caretaking and is clearly on a mission—she is usually unruffled by Mom's ups and downs.

I try to ignore the panicked, desperate feeling emanating from somewhere deep in my body. I make an attempt to reassure my sister that things will be okay, but we both know they won't—an understanding that hangs between us, unspoken, like a thick fog in the air. I decide it is time to try to be compassionate with my sister, who does occasionally drive me crazy. I even have just enough self-awareness, and admittedly it doesn't take much, to realize that it is much nicer to be hanging out in Hilton Head on a beautiful spring day than taking care of Mom in Columbus.

Sometimes when Susan starts talking she never stops, as in you can put the phone down and pick it up ten minutes later and she won't have noticed you were gone (trust me on this one). It would be enough for me to pull my hair out, if I had any left. Today my patience lasts a good half hour, even though the desperate feeling about Mom persists the entire time.

I am genuinely worried. But then fifteen minutes after I hang up, my cell phone rings again. It is Mom. She has come back to life, at least for now. She even sounds pretty good. She asks me where I am and how I am doing, and she tells me she loves me. She is as coherent as an eighty-seven-year-old Alzheimer's patient with terminal cancer can be. I take three or four deep breaths for the first time in an hour. Steve Jobs, before he died, said, "Even people who want to go to heaven don't want to die to get there." He had that Buddhist way of seeing and expressing the brutal truth. It might be equally true that no one wants their elderly mother to live a long time when she is uncomfortable and ready to go, but that doesn't mean you want her to die today.

But Mom isn't dead yet.

There's this thing about death—when you get close enough to it, it makes you think about life. Not life as an abstract concept. Your own life.

I grew up in a family that didn't think much about what might be going on below the surface or, for that matter, even recognize that there was a "below the surface." Perceptions, as in what other people thought of you, mattered more than reality. We thought of ourselves as "upper-middle class," meaning we were "above" some others.

I didn't understand back then that upper-middle class typically means that you have a savings account. Which of course, as I eventually found out, my parents did not have. When we went out to Sunday brunch my sisters Susan and Robin, who were identical twins, were always being shown off, dressed in identical clothes. My mom was a beautiful woman in her day, with looks becoming of the homecoming queen she was. My dad had his own car dealership back in the 1960s when that was a big deal ("what's good for General Motors is good for America" perhaps summarizes how big of a deal it was). He drove fancy cars and parked them next to the front door of the restaurant whenever they let him. There was a lot of "show," and even some glitz, at least glitz for the small Ohio town where we lived. Our house had two big yards on both sides, which I happily repurposed into my own mini golf course. It turns out we didn't actually own those two side yards.

Not to be too dramatic, but I was a bit of an appendage to all of this. It helped when my brother Scott was born eight years after me, especially since he literally came out of the womb with a sense of humor. But for a long time, I was not noticed, not much part of the show.

In a town where athletics was a big deal, I loved sports but wasn't much of an athlete. Actually, I was a terrible athlete. The highlight of my junior high "athletic career" was being the last guy to make the eighth-grade basketball team, but hey, don't laugh. I knocked down four points against Fostoria on the road in a hostile environment. The only way I earned my high school letter jacket—which was the only way that I ever got a date (and not many of them at that)—was by playing golf. And back then nobody but the golf team and our coach cared much about it. All everyone ever cared about was football, basketball, and baseball.

I was average-looking at best, and the glasses I've worn since I was seven didn't help. I didn't look like a jock and I didn't talk like a jock and I certainly didn't play like a jock. I just wanted to be one.

I didn't stand out in any way, shape, or form, in a place and time where standing out seemed overly important. And in a family where standing out was all that mattered. All of which I thought was a curse. And it was—until it turned out to be a blessing. Slowly, I started to search below the surface of life and beneath my parents' often superficial mindset. I began to realize that there's this thing called an inner life.

And some years after that, I discovered running. Which changed my life. Which helped me find that inner life. And which, in the end, turned me into—sort of—an actual athlete.

I'm an expert at how not to change. When I go to the same restaurant, which I often do, I order the same thing over and over again. When I figure out how to do something on the computer, I keep doing it that same way, even if everyone tells me there is a better, faster way. This is the story of how I changed, despite the odds and despite how my brain is wired not to change.

It is the story of how I changed the hard way, one marathon at a time.

1

MARATHON MARATHON

T*erre Haute, Indiana, May 1980, 3 hours, 54 minutes*

"It is better by noble boldness to run the risk of being subject to half the evils we anticipate than to remain in cowardly listlessness for fear of what might happen."
Herodotus, Greek Historian

I AM the last person you would think would have started running marathons. Nobody growing up in Bowling Green thought of marathon running as a sport. At least not until Frank Shorter won gold in the 1972 Summer Olympics marathon in Munich, and even then, running was a fringe sport. Nobody "went out for a run," or a jog, or whatever you called it back then. The cross-country team was a bunch of weirdos. Everyone knew that.

Whatever running I did was accidental. Usually I was running away from the bigger kids or running to get home in time for dinner (the only rule that my parents burdened me with, other than having to fold the grocery bags). Once I was even running from the cops, back when our idea of relieving the boredom was to throw eggs at cars. The mistake I made was that I was with my friend Greg Black, who had a good enough arm to later be drafted as a pitcher for the Detroit Tigers. He wasn't going to miss a car from twenty feet away. The egg-throwing thing was fun right up until we returned to the scene of the crime, the city park, to collect our remaining eggs. After we got caught no one, including the cops, believed my alibi, which was that I never had a chance to throw anything, even though it happened to be true.

Even now, I can't quite piece together how I started running. I lived in a frat house for a few years when I went to Miami University (the one in Ohio, not Florida). The frat house was the last in a long row of frat houses, right next to a country road leading out of town. For whatever reason, I started running every once in a while down that country road, Bonham Springs, usually in the late afternoon. I didn't even know there was such a thing as running shoes back then. I just took off, up and down the hills, one simple step at a time. I certainly didn't think of myself as a runner and I didn't do any of the typical things that runners tend to do, like write down my times in a log or even, for that matter, keep track of my time. I didn't know anything about stretching or warming up. I have no idea to this day how far I was running or how long Bonham Springs was; I turned around where it ran into the first big crossroad, and then ran back to the frat house. It might have been nervous energy—a kind phrase for anxiety—that got me started. Or maybe it was the amazingly terrible food—made by our frat house cook, Orvie, who was at least seventy years old and even took to laughing himself at how bad the food was —that I was trying to purge from my system.

I was ridiculously goal oriented back then, obsessive about lists and checking them off. What was life about other than getting things done? (Aside from that, I was a lot of fun to hang out with). When I finished running up and down that country road, I felt calm and relaxed, or at least less nervous: a kind of calm that I was not familiar with. The calm lasted for a while, and it wasn't just in my head. It sat there for some time, deep inside of me.

After I graduated from Miami I took a job with Arthur Andersen & Company in tech consulting. (For business history buffs, this was the Arthur Andersen that existed before that nasty little Enron problem.) It was a genuine revelation to me that I could actually get a good, professional job let alone keep one for a while. It paid $14,100 per year, which I thought was a lot for a twenty-two-year-old in 1978. I noticed after a while that work was actually kind of stressful. In a way that only a twenty-two-year-old could have, I thought I had made a unique discovery, like I was Christopher Columbus or something: working for a living could be hard.

I was hired by Chuck, a smooth-talking partner with a real nice office in downtown Columbus. Chuck was the kind of big-time guy that could get you (or at least me) to spill your guts out just by looking at you and nodding. He had this high-tech feature in his office, which was that when you sat down in the chair across from his desk, he could hit a hidden button and the door would close. He would then look at you and nod and say absolutely nothing, and you would spill your guts out. Whatever you were thinking; whatever scary thing was going on in your twenty-two-year-old brain. Or at least that's the way it worked for me. Every time. I got in a lot of trouble that way.

After I was working there a few months, Chuck asked me how it was going. I thought he actually wanted to know. So, I said something incredibly profound like, "You know, working all the time for a paycheck is stressful. And I'm not sleeping well. Got any ideas?" Chuck launched into a short speech, which ended with "exercise helps."

A few months later I was assigned to a project in Dayton, helping develop a financial system for a big utility company there. It wasn't exactly rocket science but it seemed like it to me, and the six staff unlucky enough to be working for me. My senior manager was a smart guy who carried himself like a combination of a military man and a business executive, with a fully upright posture and total composure. He was from West Virginia and his name was Joe Wright. (That's not his real name; some names have been changed to protect identities.) He was not exactly lacking in confidence, as in quite possibly an arrogant asshole. To me, he seemed like an older guy who was making it big; he was probably thirty years old at best. I was not a political type, but I figured spending a little time with my senior manager was not a bad idea and perhaps could even advance my career. So, summoning up all the nerve I could muster, I asked, "Hey, could we start doing regular status meetings, or maybe even just talk every once in a while?" This was met with a gruff, "Schneider, the only time I have for you is while I am working out over lunch."

It turned out that Mr. Wright's version of a workout was a four-mile run, starting at the YMCA by the river, at about a seven-minute-per-mile pace. Thus, began my running career. To my surprise, I discovered I could just about keep up with him, conduct a status meeting, and talk—all at the same time. Furthermore, I liked doing it. Mostly, I would ask short questions and Mr. Wright would bark out long answers, which worked for me because it was much easier to hold that seven-minute pace when I didn't have to talk.

I noticed that I got more work done on the afternoons when I ran during the lunch hour. Not exactly a Nobel Prize–winning insight, but it worked for me (and for Mr. Wright, who was never happier than when he was talking down to me). Then, I decided to take my running to the next level and enter a ten-mile race. As only I could, I entered the most hairbrained, foolhardy race that one could possibly come up with. It was a ten-miler on the airport runway of Wright-Patterson Air Force Base. One mile out and one mile back down the runway—five times total out and back. I wish I were exaggerating about this, but I am not. Talk about a scenic run. I ended up running it in eighty-two minutes and forty seconds: a little over eight-minute miles. Not too bad, although it was clear that I wasn't going to turn into Frank Shorter anytime soon.

That fall I went to visit friends in Minneapolis and ran ten miles or so with my friend Pete while his loyal dog ran with us the whole way. All three of us were tired at the end of that, but the next day I did a 10K race that consisted of two laps around Lake Calhoun in the middle of town. It took me a little over forty-two minutes. The city lake was gorgeous and, in September, Minneapolis was experiencing delightfully cool and pleasant weather. I even passed a bunch of people in that second loop around the lake.

I'm not one to look back nostalgically on my youth—except when I think about how I used to be able to do two hard runs back-to-back. Now *that* is something to get nostalgic about. Nostalgia alert: Once in my mid-twenties I ran ten miles hard one day and the next day I ran a 5K in Cincinnati in eighteen minutes nine seconds. On hills and on a hot Memorial Day weekend. Ridiculous. Okay, now I am done bragging for the rest of the book. Today, I cannot even think about running two days in a row, let alone running hard both days.

You may have noticed that I am able to remember my running times, more or less exactly, from races I ran forty years ago. Runners are people who like to put themselves through a bunch of tests— that's who we are. The thing is, there is no universal test for a runner. Some runners pride themselves on running even when it is 15 degrees below outside. That doesn't prove that you are a runner, it just proves that you are insane. Other runners keep daily running logs like it's the Magna Carta or some such document. Some even try to keep a streak going consisting of how many days in a row that they run (even if they have the flu, etc., etc.). In today's social media culture, I even get notified online when a faint acquaintance of mine runs an eleven-minute mile, and they are undoubtedly uploading that to some sophisticated data analytics program to assess their fitness.

During the 2012 US presidential campaign, vice presidential candidate Paul Ryan was asked in a radio interview what his finishing time was in the only marathon he ever ran: Grandma's Marathon, which takes place every June in Duluth, Minnesota. He said he ran it in a little under three hours, which is, of course, crazy fast—and, as it turns out, much faster than his true time. Somebody looked it up, and he ran it in a little under four hours. He tried to pass it off as no big deal. "Hey, I was only off an hour in remembering my time for the only marathon that I've ever run." Yeah, right. In case you are wondering whether or not you should ever trust conservative ideologue politicians, well, I think I just answered that question. Real runners remember their race times, down to the minute if not the second, no matter how long ago it was. Especially when it's your only marathon.

Having caught the bug, I decided to try my hand at an actual marathon. Have I mentioned yet that I was pretty darn goal-oriented? There are two ways to look at this. On the positive side, I was good at staying disciplined. When the partners at Arthur Andersen told me I needed to pass the CPA exam even though tech consulting had nothing to do with auditing, I took them at their word and spent every weekend for a year or so hanging out with two big orange books that taught me all I needed to know to pass the exam.

The other way to look at it, though, is that I would sign up to do wild stuff without thinking too much about it. Like spending all of my weekends for a year when I was twenty-three years old hanging out with two big orange books. Like getting married to my college girlfriend "Amy" when I was also only twenty-three. Like deciding to run a marathon when the most I had run before that was ten miles.

~

So, here I am on a warm Saturday in May 1980, running The Marathon Marathon (no, that's not a typo—it's sponsored by Marathon Oil). Of all places, the race is in Terre Haute, Indiana. I haven't been to Terre Haute before or since. The first half of the course is flat and open, but the lack of scenery and shade is made up for by passing a bunch of smelly industrial plants. Then we hit what evidently passes for scenery in Terre Haute—rolling hills followed by more smelly industrial plants. I do what all marathon runners do when they start to tire: I keep going and put one foot in front of the other. It's not a complicated sport, which means it is one I can do.

They say there are two halves to a marathon: the first 20 miles and the last 6.2. They are right. Towards the end of the race I have a hard time literally holding my head upright, so instead I look down to confirm I am still alive by observing that my feet are moving. Which they barely are. Which is not such a great sign.

The best thing about the Marathon Marathon at the end is that it is over, finally. And I have done something that, however modest, is perhaps even athletic: I have run 26.2 miles pretty much without stopping...other than those few water stops towards the end that I stretched into leisure walks. The second-best thing is that I can now eat all that I want, since in my warped mind I have burned enough calories to earn the food. I know that's weird, but I can't seem to change that part of myself. I am the kind of guy who thinks of vacations as something you "earn."

The night of the marathon, I celebrate by going to the wedding of a good friend of mine. Which sounds like a great way to celebrate, except that both the wedding and the reception take place at some evangelical church where there is much chanting involved, not much food, and no alcohol.

Nevertheless, my marathon running career is off to a start. Even if it did start in Terre Haute.

~

WE NEVER KNOW exactly why we choose to spend our time in life in the ways that we do, or at least I didn't. But there was a simplicity to the act of running that appealed to me. You don't need any special equipment, which works in my case because to say that I am "frugal" is much kinder than the truth. You can run from anywhere you are in the world, at least in the United States. And, most importantly in my case, you don't need anyone else to do it with. Like most kids, I was good at inventing my own games when I was growing up, and certainly making up the rules. I didn't need a friend to compete with, although it was okay when one was around. When I was learning to play golf, I was Jack Nicklaus with one ball and Arnie Palmer with the other. Enough imagination could make up for any kind of boredom. Running offers a chance to recreate a more grown-up version of those childhood fantasies.

Now that I think about it, the seeds of my running career just might have been sown even earlier in my life. One of the great parts of growing up in Bowling Green was that it was a college town. For a sports-obsessed kid, this meant a whole bunch of sporting events to attend, even beyond the "mainstream" sports of football and basketball. When the university built an ice arena, suddenly we had a nationally-ranked ice hockey team that actually competed with basketball for our mindshare. We had ice shows featuring a little kid a year younger than me, Scott Hamilton (who went on to win gold in men's skating at the 1984 Olympics). Heck, we even had a curling rink, a sport that I always think of as shuffleboard on ice.

We also had a strong university track team, featuring an NCAA champion steeplechaser named Sid Sink. The steeplechase is that weird race where you jump over hurdles into a puddle that you can't possibly clear, and then run a long way and collapse at the finish. We all thought Sid Sink would be an Olympian. But then in late 1971, another guy emerged from obscurity on our track team. He was a miler named Dave Wottle, a mild-mannered guy from Canton, Ohio. All of a sudden Wottle was running world-class times in the mile. He qualified for the Munich Olympics in the 800 meters, which is a little less than a half mile.

There's a great broadcast of the 800-meters 1972 Munich Olympics finals that you can find on YouTube, with Jim McKay on the call and Marty Liquori as the color commentator. (McKay would become famous a few days after the event for staying on air for many hours as much of the Israeli Olympic team was gunned down by Palestinian terrorists.) I know about the YouTube video only because I have watched it about 5,000 times. Dave Wottle runs the first lap so slow that about halfway around the track Marty Liquori wonders out loud if he is injured. He is in last place by some significant distance. But then he starts catching up to the back of the pack on the second and last lap. With a quarter of the race to go, he is moving up but still nearly in last position. But now he is running with ease while the leaders are showing the strain of going out so fast. Wottle is the skinny white guy wearing a golf cap to keep the hair out of his eyes.

In the last 100 meters he passes four guys, as McKay calls the race, "He's got one Kenyan. He's got the second Kenyan. Can he do it?" Wottle beats the last guy he needs to pass, a Russian runner who had not lost in two years, at the tape by the tip of his cap. No matter how many times I watch this race, it still sends chills up my spine. And no matter how many times I watch it, it's impossible to believe Wottle is going to win the race until he actually does.

In reality, Wottle actually ran a great tactical race. A more careful review of the footage reveals that even though it looks like he started out incredibly slow at the beginning, in reality he ran an even pace the entire time. What happened was the guys at the front of the pack went out too fast and then tightened up and faded down the stretch. Wottle looks stunned when he wins the race, but he might have been the least surprised guy in the stadium. Dave Wottle taught me something that stuck. I learned to value steady and consistent effort—and to always have a strategy.

After Wottle won that gold medal, we had a big parade for him on Main Street and I wore a T-shirt emblazoned with the legend "Wottletown USA"; the picture made it into the *BG Sentinel-Tribune* daily newspaper, which may as well as have been the *New York Times* as far as I was concerned. Then, miraculously, Dave Wottle showed up the next year as my student teacher in my favorite class, American History, taught by the fantastic Esther Hayhurst. Dave was everything you could want in an Olympic hero—soft-spoken, modest, nice, smart, and with the lean-runner look down pat. Nothing was ever cooler than the day that he brought his gold medal to class and we passed it around.

Who knows what Dave's story and actually meeting him and holding that gold medal for a few seconds did to my fragile eighteen-year-old mind? I know it made a dent. Maybe it's why the rest of my life I have loved comebacks, and always connected my running to coming back from whatever misfortune I might be working through at the time.

About thirty-five years later, I am in the office of my genuinely insane podiatrist in Cincinnati, Dr. Osborne. Dr. Osborne was a good high school and college miler and cross-country runner. He still holds many Norwood High School cross-country records; if you don't know that when you walk into his office, I promise you will by the time you leave. I visit Dr. Osborne regularly because in addition to him being genuinely insane I, as an aging runner, have many foot and toe issues and he happens to be a fabulous foot doctor...who knows enough never to recommend the therapy of taking a few days off from running.

Dr. Osborne claims to have run several races in college against Dave Wottle, a claim that I have no easy way to verify, but I believe him. He is not a guy who spins anything, more the type that hits you between the eyeballs with whatever he wants to say. In other words, Dr. Osborne has no filters. I'm trying to take a mid-size software company public and everything, including four hundred people's jobs, is on the line. Dr. Osborne seems to understand this as well as a genuinely insane podiatrist can. He knows it's important, he knows that people's jobs are on the line, and he knows I stand to make some real money if it works. He responds with his regular dose of bad jokes (most of which can't be aired on prime time), and almost incidentally does some stuff to my toes. As he chases me out the door, he says, "I know you are going to get this IPO done. I know you are going to pull a Dave Wottle and take it at the tape."

It was the perfect description of what I wanted and needed to do. In this world you need to take emotional support from wherever you can get it, even genuinely insane podiatrists.

2

GLASS CITY MARATHON

T oledo, Ohio, September 1981, 3 hours, 51 minutes

"Life is what happens to you while you're busy making other plans."
John Lennon, "Beautiful Boy (Darling Boy)"

EVENTUALLY I DECIDED that I needed to leave Arthur Andersen, even though I was doing well at the firm. After one year, I got a promotion to senior staff consultant that usually didn't happen until after two or three years. Just to fully demonstrate the level of maturity that I had reached by the time I made senior staff consultant and the wisdom inherent in that promotion, I celebrated this career advance in Dayton with my good friend Kevin from Bowling Green by going out to TGI Fridays, drinking way too many Long Island Iced Teas, going home and lying in bed while the room swirled around, and getting into work the next day at 1:00 p.m. Everyone knew why and I was a little embarrassed, in addition to not feeling so great. Clearly, I was well-equipped to handle such newfound responsibilities.

I decided to leave Arthur for a couple of reasons. Firstly, all the partners in Columbus were conservative men with a narrow view of the world. Most of them lived in Upper Arlington. I didn't want to be like them when I grew up, whenever that turned out to be. But more importantly, my first wife, Amy (not her real name), hated the firm. She was what my dad liked to call "a women's libber," and thought the whole place was sexist. She was quite correct about all of that, but she might have missed the fact that my paycheck was paying her PhD program tuition—or at least that's how I remember it.

I soon realized my marriage wasn't working out too well but I didn't understand why. I was trying to use my parents' marriage as a model, having no other models available to me and not yet understanding any of the imperfections of their particular union. Nothing was working. In my clueless state and unable to accept blame, I hatched the idea of leaving Arthur Andersen, going back to school to get a PhD, and living the grad student life with Amy. I decided to enroll in a graduate economics program to pick up the required courses and then try to get into a top-notch PhD program in economics, and then convince Amy to move with me to get her PhD, hopefully at the same school. I figured all this would help us patch things back together, since we would be students together again and there would be no Arthur Andersen in the picture to drive her nuts. What could possibly go wrong with this four-bank pool shot?

In the winter of 1981, I gave Arthur Andersen nine months' notice and let my boss know that I planned to return to grad school that fall. The nine-month notice thing might have been more appropriate if I was, for example, the CEO of the company, but I had a perhaps exaggerated sense of ethics back in those days and almost certainly an exaggerated sense of self-importance. I also didn't understand the concept of leverage, as in as soon as I told my bosses I was leaving I would have none left for the remaining nine months when I still needed a paycheck. But I plunged ahead with my plan anyway.

As soon as I told them I was leaving in nine months, they moved me onto a project in Montreal, Canada, rather than keeping me on a project in Dayton, so that I could see Amy during the week. Which may or may not have doomed the marriage I was then trying to save. Arthur's big "give" was that they would get me home every weekend, which was easier said than done. There were no direct flights between Montreal and Cincinnati, I had to be in Montreal the whole week, and there were border customs to deal with in each direction. (US customs back then was no big deal, but Canadian customs in Montreal on a busy Sunday night was an entirely different story.) There were several Sunday nights when I planted myself with book on a USAir flight from Cincinnati to Buffalo to Hamilton, Ontario, before finally heading for Montreal. I was certainly the only person who got on the plane in Cincinnati and stayed all the way until Montreal. Thank goodness I liked to read.

There were actually some benefits to Montreal, despite the state of my marriage and even given that I started on the project in the middle of January. For one thing, the city sits on an island above the St. Lawrence River, and back then there was a gritty urban vibrancy to the city unlike anywhere I had ever been before. It was credibly the most European city in North America, so being there was like being in Europe. At least, at age twenty-three I could not tell the difference. It also happened to be a truly great city to run in. My corporate apartment was situated within a few blocks of the old Montreal Forum (where the Canadiens famously played hockey), about a half mile from McGill University, and only a mile from my office. I walked the mile down St. Lawrence Street even in the dead of winter, except when prudence took over and I took the subway system, which was excellent. Most importantly, I was close to the foot of Mount Royal, the old fortress-turned-city-park that was a steep climb for at least one mile from where I lived to get to the top. The reward for a normal person was a beautiful view of the city when you summited. The reward for an obsessive runner was a hard workout that could be achieved quickly so you could still get to work more or less on time.

Nearly every morning during the week I took off on a viciously hard charge up Mount Royal. Sometime in early 1981 I decided it would be a good idea to run another marathon after I left Arthur Andersen, and that Montreal and Mount Royal would be a good training ground for my second stab at the race. The fact that winter was finally disappearing from Montreal didn't hurt. There is nothing better to an obsessive runner than discovering a new city by running through every neighborhood within striking distance, and that's how I came to know Montreal.

After enough morning runs up Mount Royal, I signed up for the Glass City Marathon in Toledo, Ohio, in September 1981, which happened to fall on the weekend after my last day of work for Arthur Andersen. I dragged Amy up to Toledo and we stayed with my Grandma Gerry at her house in Toledo. Grandma Gerry was a truly unique character and one thing for sure was that she loved a good story. Whether or not the story was factual was of only marginal concern, as her late-life career as a "society page journalist"—which consisted of telling stories about parties that she may or may not have attended—seemed to prove.

~

MY GLASS CITY Marathon race provides plenty of real-life material for Grandma Gerry to work with. Unbelievably, it is over 90 degrees at 7:00 a.m. in Toledo in the middle of September. Who could have planned for that? To make matters worse, the race is delayed for a half hour or so by the rather inconvenient event of a train coming through the race course. A train never being a great thing for a pack of time-obsessed runners to maneuver around, the brilliant race organizers delay the race—ensuring that it is even hotter by the time we begin.

I'm in pretty good shape, or at least I think so during the first five miles, so I get off to a nice start. But eventually the heat bears down on me. My walks through the water stops grow progressively longer as the race goes on. I notice that there aren't many cheering spectators standing out in the 92-degree heat, and in fact most of the spectators aren't actually moving. I suspect they are still alive but I am not entirely sure. My stride starts wobbling around mile eighteen. I forget about anything or anyone else and concentrate on putting one foot in the front of the other. The Buddhists say pain is mandatory but suffering is optional, and I am beginning to understand what they mean. Pushing myself to the next telephone pole starts out as a game, but before long it is mental combat of the first order.

By mile twenty-two, I am mostly walking and feeling woozy. A kid with a water hose is hosing down all the runners who pass by. As I stagger past, he asks me in a voice that sounds a little too innocent, "Why are you walking while everyone else is running?" I am positive he understands exactly what he is saying, but I don't have the energy to chase the stupid kid as he runs away laughing.

I manage the last six miles with the combo of running and walking that will later characterize my finishing miles in several of my marathons. The running isn't even running but more of a "marathon shuffle." Somehow, I manage to get across the finish line in three hours and fifty-one minutes, or three minutes faster than my first marathon. Having accomplished my goal of beating this time I am happy, but it turns out the adventure is only just beginning.

I lie down in the grass and start stretching, beginning by pulling one of my legs up into my chest while lying on my back. This seems like what you are supposed to do, from watching other runners. Massive leg cramp. I address this situation maturely by screaming loudly in pain. This earns me the right be to dragged over to a medic tent. Somebody starts pouring water down my throat and takes my blood pressure, which turns out to be rather low: 70/50. This is not viewed as an acceptable number by the doctor at the scene. He orders someone to keep pouring water down me and give it five minutes and then take my blood pressure again. Five minutes later, I feel a little better but my blood pressure remains the same. Whereupon the doctor looks at my then twenty-four-year-old wife and says, "I'm sorry. We are going to have to take your father to the hospital." And I am all of twenty-five, although admittedly I don't have much hair and she has a bit of a baby face. I start laughing but she fails to find the humor in the situation. I think she might have been upset about the whole "Let's drive four hours to Toledo and four hours back so my idiot husband can run a marathon in 90-degree heat" thing, but my memory gets a little foggy here.

Clearly, the trip to the emergency room is going to be an unwanted diversion for both of us. Amy wants to get back to her studies—and, quite possibly, away from me. And I want to avoid the embarrassment of needing a medical intervention to resume the rest of my life.

About the time I get put on a stretcher and am loaded into the ambulance, it occurs to me that I declined to extend my health insurance on my last day of work, which was two days ago. Even in my compromised condition, I am coherent enough to ask the medic at hand how much the ambulance ride is going to cost. He declines to answer on the basis of the fact that I am lying on a stretcher in a somewhat precarious state. Finally, I pry the answer out of him, which is something like $300 for a five-minute ride. I'm not exactly flush with cash, having just left my $26K-per-year job for the life of a grad student. At this point, I suggest that we stop the ambulance ride and I drive myself to the emergency room, thank you very much. This request is met with a mix of laughter and derision that adds up to me needing to lie back down on the stretcher and try to enjoy the $60-per-minute ride.

Things are calm in the emergency room, at least much calmer than either Amy or Grandma Gerry. It turns out that I am not actually dying, although by this point Amy has called Grandma Gerry at her house, who has called my parents in Arizona, who have called my Uncle Dale at his cottage on Lake Erie and instructed him to terminate his leisurely Sunday afternoon and drive forty-five minutes to pay me a visit in the ER. Uncle Dale doesn't even know that I am running a marathon in Toledo that weekend until he gets this panicked call from my parents. Uncle Dale is not happy to learn this and is especially grumpy about having to get up from the couch on his outdoor patio and leave his cottage. By the time he and my aunt arrive, I am perfectly fine—I've taken in a couple bags of fluids via a nice nurse and an IV—all of which seems to add to Uncle Dale's surly mood. I hop in the car with Amy and head home to Oxford, Ohio.

~

DESPITE THE FINANCIAL and familial implications, I was happy about finishing another marathon and especially about beating my time from my first marathon. However, as it turned out, Amy didn't share my happiness about any of this. In a word, she was pissed. And probably for good reason, since from her point of view I dragged her away for the weekend, only to run 26.2 miles in 92-degree heat and end up at the emergency room. Even I could see this might not have been the best of weekends for her. It was a quiet and unpleasant ride back to Oxford.

If I had any question about whether or not my marriage was in trouble, that question was soon answered in the affirmative. I have always been allergic to cats. One day I returned to my apartment to find two cats there, and they didn't belong to the neighbors. When I asked Amy why they were there and how I was supposed to live with them, it soon became clear that the cats outranked me in the household hierarchy. In fact, it was clear right then and there that I was in the process of being replaced.

Amy had been in therapy for a while, which I knew and I was fine with that. What I didn't fully understand was that I was the primary subject/villain of the therapy sessions. One day, at her request, I went to visit the therapist with Amy. As soon as I got there it became evident that it was my job to defend myself to both Amy and the therapist, and that I had already been tried and convicted in absentia. There was little I could say to change the trajectory of this dire situation; actually, there was nothing I could say. Amy told the therapist she would be happier if I wasn't there.

I processed exactly what this meant quickly. We left the therapist's office and wandered up the Slant Walk between the university and the small town of Oxford. We stopped at Burger King for lunch, the terrible food there being perfectly aligned with my terrible mood. We were both crying. I wasn't—obviously—overly perceptive about what was going on in my young marriage, but I did understand that it was time to go. And I did have some pride left. So, I packed up my stuff into my car and drove down to Cincinnati, to my friend Tom Morgan's apartment. It was time to sleep on the couch—any couch of any friend would have done that night. Tom helpfully suggested that we dine at a cafeteria eloquently named the Cambridge Inn. Other than the fact that I hate cafeterias and that the average age of the patrons had to be approaching eighty, it was a fun dinner.

The demise of my first marriage hit me like a ton of bricks. I was paralyzed mentally, physically, even spiritually. I couldn't think too well, I could hardly move, I couldn't concentrate on anything, and I certainly couldn't sleep. There is something about your first life crisis —or at least there was about mine—that is unforgettable in a unique way. Fundamentally, I was not at all sure I would get through it.

My parents had a relationship that later on I learned had its complications and difficult times, but even with much more history in the books they shared a deeply close bond. It was also superficially idyllic, and unfortunately, I wasn't too far beyond that superficial view of relationships at age twenty-five. I had modeled, or tried to model, my marriage on my parents' relationship. I was in love with the idea of being in love, but I didn't understand that you can't force that. Things have to be natural. The more adulation and affection Amy wanted from me, the harder it was for me to genuinely feel affection or adulation. I thought that happy couples don't argue with each other, which is, of course, ridiculous. So, we buried our problems, never expressed our anger in a productive way, and naturally, that only made everything worse. I couldn't even manage to tell her that I hated going shopping at the mall on Sunday afternoons when the Browns were playing on TV. And that was way back when the Browns were a good team.

It wasn't just that my marriage was broken, as bad as that was: it seemed that nearly everything I believed about life—and especially about myself—was wrong. I was massively at fault for much of what had gone wrong in the relationship, a fact about which Amy, with help from her therapist, could wax eloquent. The truth was that towards the end of our relationship, I was looking forward to the long plane flight to Montreal with several connecting flights. I was looking forward to being buried in my books, to escaping from the rest of life, which those trips gave me an excuse to do. I started out running marathons to get healthier and to relieve stress, but in the end running for hours at a time had turned into something else. It had turned into a way to escape the problems in what was then the most important relationship in my life. It was actually not a completely destructive escape hatch, but it was an escape hatch nonetheless. Yet as massively at fault as I was, the demise of that marriage didn't rest entirely on my shoulders. It took me months to figure that out.

In the meantime, I was woefully disoriented. I was going to grad school at the University of Cincinnati (UC) in economics, but I stopped going to class. I couldn't sleep—mostly, I would lie in bed trying to figure out what just happened in my life. This wasn't supposed to be happening to me. I was supposed to have a wife and kids and good job and all that stuff. It wasn't part of my life plan to divorce at twenty-five and be replaced by two ugly cats. I thought this was supposed to happen to other people, not me. If only I knew what was yet to come.

I somehow managed to get through my classes at UC by first giving all of my professors what was a credible enough sob story to be able to defer my final exams until after the Christmas break. This was important, as in several classes the grade on the final exam comprised 100 percent of my grade for the entire course. Over Christmas I visited my parents at their condo complex in Newport Beach, California. Mom and Dad never had any money after they left Bowling Green, and maybe not even before they left Bowling Green, but that didn't stop them from living in some rather nice digs in some significantly upscale towns. Only over time did it become clear that they managed money about as well as teenagers with stolen credit cards.

Eventually, I managed to start sleeping again. I even started running again. When I couldn't sleep I thought that meant I was too tired to run. But it turned out I had that backwards—I only started sleeping *after* I started running and became physically tired. Every day that Christmas break in Newport Beach I would run down to the Pacific Coast at sundown and then back to my parents' condo, about a four-mile round trip.

An analytical person, I tend to complicate things. Now the simple act of putting one foot in front of the other until I reached the ocean began to heal me. I would reach the ocean quickly; it was mostly downhill for two miles and I had lost some weight, unintentionally, because I was so wired and strung out. It was a fast and easy run down to that ocean, and breathing deeply and running easily was what I needed. When I arrived, I walked the two blocks along the ocean hoping for the healing power of nature to work its magic, trying to sort out my life, and then I ran back up the hill to the condo. Running was literally putting life back into me.

My dad, who died nine years ago, was not an analytical person. He didn't think deeply about much. But he cared about his kids and occasionally he would blurt out some good advice. Perhaps the kind of advice you get only from lived experience. He said to me about my marriage (pretending that it was my choice), "Just get back into it or get out of it, but don't spend months going back and forth about it." I realized, at whatever odds, he had tripped over something important.

After the Christmas break, I boarded a plane from LAX back to Cincinnati. To my amazement, I aced all of my economic exams. For the next six months, it was enough that the sun came up every day. I was alive and I was making it through. The more I ran, the better I felt. Every time I had to take an exam in grad school, I ran before-hand—hard—often doing intervals on the indoor track at the University of Cincinnati. Every time I did this, running cleared my head and calmed me down. I thought better after I ran. For the rest of my time as a student, I ran before every exam.

I started to get in good shape, at least by my standards. There was a local running shop, run by an ex-running coach named Bob Roncker, that was making a name for itself (and selling a lot of running shoes) by sponsoring 10K races at Lunken Airport, the private airport on the east side of Cincinnati with a bike path and golf course surrounding it. I was running six-minute-plus miles in those races without much of a problem. I still have a few pictures of myself from that period. I had very little body fat, a mustache that everyone said made me look gay, and I looked lean but not mean. One Saturday I ran thirty-eight minutes twenty-one seconds in a 10K, which was fast for me. It didn't hurt too much. In fact, I liked the fact that it hurt a little, since I've always bought into the whole no-pain/no-gain thing.

My life changed irrevocably during those six months. I got into some great econ PhD programs—Wisconsin, Stanford, Chicago; took a job managing software programmers at a small tech company in Cincinnati to make some dough before grad school; loved the job enough to think about staying a while; decided not to get a PhD in econ after all . . . and met the woman of my dreams. All crammed into those six months. Now that I think about it, there just might have been some connection between meeting the woman of my dreams and deciding to stay in town.

3

AVENUE OF THE GIANTS MARATHON

H*umboldt County, California, May 1985, 3 hours, 47 minutes, 17 seconds*

"Out there in the wild, on a long journey, you hike your own hike, blaze your own trail, and only you can find what you're looking for."
Scott Jurek, North: Finding My Way While Running the Appalachian Trail

I ENDED up working for a few years in Cincinnati and then I decided to study for an MBA full-time. I'd like to have an elegant explanation for why I chose this route, but the truth is I just didn't know what else to do with myself. I knew a lot more about what I didn't want to do than what I did want to do. I knew I didn't want to get a PhD in economics; there were (and still are) just too many smart economists who didn't agree with each other on anything. Plus, economics was becoming quantitative and I was skeptical that the world's problems could be reduced down to a math equation (and that's still true too). I knew I didn't want to get an MBA part-time; I took a few evening courses at the University of Cincinnati, but I was never very good at multi-processing work and school. And I definitely knew that I didn't want to just keep working a small software company in Cincinnati.

I've always had a sense of adventure. My dad wasn't anywhere near perfect, but he helped bake that sense of adventure into who I am. Many parents focus on telling you what you can't do rather than what you can do. But when I was eighteen years old and I asked my dad if I could borrow a car from his used car lot to go camping out west for a month with two of my friends, he simply said yes. And when, the night before we were supposed to leave, we busted the glass window in the rear-side of that convertible while packing the car, he didn't get mad at me but instead got it fixed before we left town. I'm not even sure he asked me what day we would be back. He knew I would find my way home.

Ready for a new life adventure, I applied to a bunch of MBA programs across the country. My testing scores (GMAT) were strong, because I was always good at taking tests. I could scrounge up excellent personal references and, pre-Enron, Arthur Andersen had positive name recognition. Furthermore, the MBA programs liked people with a few years' work experience, and I had five years of actually working for a paycheck by then. I ended up getting into every program that I applied to, including Stanford, which was then the top-rated program in the country. When I opened the letter of acceptance and agreed to go to Stanford, which I remember like it was yesterday, I thought it was a big deal—I hadn't yet learned the lesson that I should already have learned from running—that when you climb one hill there is always another, usually bigger, hill right over the horizon.

I packed all of my stuff, or most of it, into my red Pontiac T-1000, with my ten-speed bike strapped onto the hatchback. I left the rest of my belongings at the house of my girlfriend, Elaine, who was staying in Cincinnati with her eight-year old son, Rik. Elaine and I got along great. We had met two years before in a class recommended to me by the senior minister of a large church, Hyde Park United Methodist Church, who also happened to be the father of one of my best friends. Dr. Bichsel explained that his church had a large Sunday night group for separated and divorced people. At first, I couldn't imagine meeting a great girlfriend in a church group, but I turned out to be very wrong about that. We met in a class called Growing Through Divorce, which had the fascinating ratio of about ten women for each man. Almost all of the women were crying because their husbands had left them and they weren't sure what to do next; Elaine was the one who was not crying.

Elaine and I promised each other a long-distance relationship, but we both knew the odds of that working between Cincinnati and Palo Alto for two years weren't all that great. Even though technically I still had an apartment in a down-and-out part of Clifton with a married couple, by then we had lived together at her place for two years. Although when she asked me to do housework, I tried to classify myself as "just a guest."

Even though Elaine and I got along great, there was a problem. Her ex-husband was nearly the textbook definition of a disastrous ex-spouse, who also happened to be a big-shot lawyer in Chicago. There was no way we were going to pull off moving Elaine and Rik to California over her ex-husband's objections, so we didn't try. Plus, Elaine had a job she needed to support herself and Rik, and I needed to figure out how to get through Stanford business school academically, which I had realized would not be a slam dunk.

So, I headed west solo in August 1984. My now ex-employer had been kind enough to help fund part of my trip by asking me to stop and see a client of theirs, the Federal Aviation Administration (FAA), in Oklahoma City. Our system kept track of all of the documentation for each airplane for the FAA, indexed by that little code that you can easily see on the front driver's side of a small airplane. I'm not sure exactly what I did for the client during that trip but I did get reimbursed for a bunch of travel expenses, and I do vividly remember watching Joan Benoit win the first Olympic women's marathon in Los Angeles while I was there. I sat in my Oklahoma City hotel room, glued to the television. She led from wire-to-wire, running down a closed LA freeway in a white baseball cap not unlike Dave Wottle's golf cap from 1972. If you didn't get chills up your spine when she ran into the Los Angeles Memorial Coliseum leading the marathon with one lap to go, you were not human and you certainly were not an American. And you definitely weren't a runner.

I kept heading west, staying overnight with my friend Kevin who was then living in a suburb of Dallas. He was working a good job and he had one of those fancy refrigerators, which seemed to me at the time to embody the good life. It occurred to me that my future was much more uncertain than his, and getting an MBA would eat up my life savings (then $30K) and put me in debt on top of that. But I was betting on myself, which is maybe the best kind of bet to take when you are young. I tried not to think about it all too much as I turned up the music in my Pontiac, at least until I hit the part of New Mexico where there are no FM radio stations. I passed through Flagstaff, Arizona, and kept driving until I hit Barstow, California, on the edge of the Mojave Desert. My Pontiac T-1000 was doing fine—it wouldn't break down until I repeated the same trip the following year—and back then all I needed was a Wendy's or Pizza Hut to keep me going. When I felt lonely I would, pathetically, chat up whoever was working the counter at Wendy's. Every morning I would wake up and run three or four miles before I hopped into my car to drive as many miles as I could. A simple equation. I finally arrived in Paso Robles, California, where I-40 runs into 101 North. 101 North was like hitting the promised land to me. The desert was in my rearview mirror. My future was somewhere out the front window—a bit fuzzy, but the horizon was wide and long.

When I got to Stanford, they threw me into a dorm room for a few days, since my "permanent accommodations" weren't quite ready. My permanent accommodations turned out to be a trailer with incredibly thin walls and two other grad students. Relationships with the opposite sex, at least discreet ones, were more or less out of the question, given the thin walls of the trailer. That was the bad news; the good news was that the trailer was right smack dab in the middle of

Stanford's campus where, as long as it wasn't the January monsoon season, the odds were good the weather would be fantastic.

The first roommate that I met was a guy named Chris from Boston, who was in the screenwriting program. I was glad that he wasn't in the business school as I figured, correctly as it turned out, I would get enough of those obnoxiously arrogant personalities in my classes. Chris and I became fast friends, even though we were not much alike. He was going to be a screenwriter and I was going to be a business guy. He was a fully urbanized Boston native and I was from Ohio. He smoked dope and I didn't. But we connected on some things, mostly the fact that we were both huge sports fans. We liked to watch *Nightline* with Ted Koppel on ABC together at 11:30 p.m. and then exchange views on the state of the world.

I learned a bunch of stuff from Chris that turned out to be useful later in life. First thing every morning he went up the student union and bought two newspapers. Then he sat at the table in the trailer and read them in their entirety, presumably to avoid working on his screenplay (something he managed to procrastinate over the entire year, since he never actually finished it.) Not being the most flexible person, it had never occurred to me that it was okay to read more than one newspaper in the morning—it just seemed decadent—but since I met Chris, it's become a lifelong habit. We both lived on almost nothing. Chris proved that one could exist for an entire year on three different foods, period. Spaghetti, cornflakes, and yogurt, washed down with Earl Grey tea.

We were both extremely competitive and we somehow managed to channel that directly into our friendship. It started with NFL football, when he suggested that we bet on each game, with the grand prize being a pizza at the end of the year. It turned out to be mostly about honor and respect, rather than pizza. It certainly wasn't going to be about money, since neither of us had any of that. Chris beat me that first year, something he never failed to remind me about for the rest of the school year. As in, literally, he found a way to mention it every time we walked past each other in that small trailer. Somewhat unbelievably, we have kept the contest going every year since (except one), for well over thirty years, and I have definitely won more years than I've lost. A fact that I remind him of more than is socially appropriate.

As if the NFL games weren't enough to bet on, he then challenged me to a one-mile race, knowing that he couldn't beat me in a marathon. He won that first one-mile race handily. But the next year, when he was living in LA, he flew up to Palo Alto for the weekend and late one Saturday afternoon we went out to the track at Palo Alto High School. We shook hands and at the start I took off in a sprint, building a quarter-of-a-lap lead for most the first three laps. But on the last lap I started to tighten up, not to mention I was totally out of breath. It felt like I had been shot. He started to try to pass me on the backstretch, but there was a puddle in the second lane and he couldn't get past. As we came down the stretch, I threw a couple of elbows to make sure and I beat him at the tape. I ended up running a 5:33 mile. He ended up a second behind me. Male honor can be a big motivator.

We challenged each other in every way we could, including who could get to all fifty states first. One weekend when flights were cheap and he was still living in LA he flew to Fargo, North Dakota, just to knock off another state. There was a big high-school basketball tournament in Fargo in the winter—who would have imagined that when they left sunny LA for Fargo—and the only place he could get a hotel room was a Motel 6. And the only thing he could figure out to do in Fargo was smoke dope in that crummy Motel 6. Then, after he got married, he actually took his wife Karen to the American South on their honeymoon simply to knock off a bunch more states. (I'm not sure he ever disclosed to his new wife exactly why they were spending their honeymoon in Jackson, Mississippi.) He got off to an early lead, but I got to the fifty states first—when I was fifty years old —mostly because he had three kids and I didn't. I closed the deal when I went to Alaska and ran a half marathon in Anchorage.

As well as Chris and I got along, there were still some knotty issues for me to deal with at Stanford. The first was that my parents were now renting a dumpy duplex apartment about ninety miles

south of Palo Alto in a town called Salinas. My dad had a car dealership back in Ohio but he had to sell the business in 1979, basically
because he was out of cash. The economy and the gas shortage didn't
help anything. Dad was always good at selling cars, but not so good at
actually running a business. There was this whole thing about
keeping track of expenses and trying to generate a profit and positive
cash flow that more or less escaped him. After the sale of his business, my parents moved to Scottsdale, Arizona, and then to California. This started a sequence whereby they needed to borrow money
from my sisters and me on a semi-regular basis. The magnitude of
their financial problems varied over time, but there were always
problems and some story behind them.

The particular problem when I was at Stanford was that my dad
had sold his car dealership for $100K, but he only got $50K down and
the guy who bought the business never paid him the other $50K. But,
of course, the buyer, some guy named Brad, still took a tax deduction
on the money he didn't pay. Naturally, the IRS was looking for the
other $50K in income they thought my dad had gotten and should
have reported. My parents were lost when it came to financial stuff,
perhaps by design, so they dragged me into the case. More than once
while I was in my first quarter at Stanford I made the three-hour
round-trip drive down to Salinas to go with my dad to meet with the
IRS. Not a fun thing to do even if you have plenty of time, which I
didn't. My parents asked me to talk to their accountant back in Ohio
to help unravel this particular quagmire. When I called him, the first
thing I learned was that they had never paid him any money, so there
were limits as to how helpful he was going to be, even though he said
he really liked my parents.

Whenever Dad and I met with the IRS, he would immediately tell
the agent that he had no clue what the IRS was talking about and he
couldn't imagine why they wanted more money from him. Then he
would tell them that if they wanted to throw him in jail they could,
since he had no money to pay them. Then he would offer to go across
the street and buy the IRS agent a black coffee, which was a clear
ruse to get out of the meeting and make me deal with everything. In a

strange, street-smart way it was actually all pretty effective. My dad and I eventually convinced the IRS that they were barking up the wrong tree, or at least a dead tree. That Christmas Eve my parents received a present from the IRS: a letter telling them they were off the hook.

The second and even bigger problem that first year at Stanford had to do with my girlfriend Elaine back in Cincinnati. I was committed to the relationship and keeping it going, but that was hard for her to process, given that I had moved 2,500 miles away. She felt abandoned and she was rather irritated. My position was that I had told her all along I was going to go to business school, but I was learning that rational logic does not necessarily override emotion when it comes to such matters, especially when the matters involve the opposite sex. So, she started dating another guy after I left town. I tried to talk to Chris about it, but after about ten minutes he simply said, in reference to her dating that other guy, that "actions speak louder than words." That was his version of emotional support.

Elaine and I eventually patched things together, which was helped by me flying back to Cincinnati every time I got a break from school and by many long, long-distance phone calls (back when such things were expensive.) I was afraid to marry a second time and it seemed like Elaine was mad at me the whole time I was at Stanford. But she was confident we belonged together. So, we ended up getting engaged. Turns out she was right and I was wrong.

It was a generally stressful time for me at Stanford, in part because I didn't know exactly why I was there. For one thing, I already knew a lot about many of the traditional business school subjects when I arrived, especially accounting and economics. I placed out of several "core" courses, which didn't reduce the number of classes I had to take but it did mean that I could substitute more interesting courses for the boring ones, like cost accounting. When I explained all this to one of my professors he said, "It almost makes one wonder why you needed to come to business school." Which wasn't a helpful comment, since I was already there and I didn't have an answer for why. Beyond not knowing why I was there, I also had no idea what I was going to do when I got out. Other than that, I had my life all sorted out.

I also had enormous trouble sleeping when at school, often showing up for my first class having hardly slept at all the night before. This turned out to be a lifelong problem that only improved late in my career when I finally learned that I could function okay without sleep, even if I was in a less-than-great mood that day. I have a theory that everyone processes about the same amount of stress: it just manifests itself in uniquely personal ways. Not sleeping well was how stress made its unwanted appearance in my life.

Running was the one thing at Stanford that was guaranteed to pull me out of a funk. By then, I already regarded running as a way out of nearly any life problem. It may not always work perfectly, but for me it would always work to a high degree—at least to deal with daily stress. And I was starting to figure out that daily stress has a way of becoming weekly stress, which has a way of becoming whole life stress. Running was not always perfect but it was the one thing that was reliable. And I was often in desperate need of reliability. It's just hard for me to be in a bad mood after I've run three or four miles, even if I try to be.

There is an elegant, minimalist simplicity to running. Running coexists well with a personality type like mine, that values hard work and discipline. The same part of me that would say to Elaine when we took a three-day weekend, "Gosh, I've earned this weekend off." There is another part of me that knows that is screwed up, but I cannot rid myself of the feeling that I am supposed to earn any fun. Elaine thinks my ancestors were Puritans.

The simplicity comes in part from the logistics of running, which are elementary-school basic. You lace up your shoes, you walk out the door, you head in a certain direction, you put one foot in front of the other, and you start breathing deeper than normal. That's about it. I've never watched a video of myself running, and I've never asked anyone else how I look while running. I've never had a running coach, and I've never thought about getting one. In my foggy memory, perhaps in the first three months of running I had to think about things a bit until my body got used to running, but since then I have given it very little thought. My body taught itself how to run. And now I simply run whenever and wherever I am able.

I didn't go to business school in Palo Alto because it was a great place to run, but if I had been looking for a great place to run I could not have picked a better one. Other than a few weeks of monsoonal rain in the winter, the weather was almost always cool enough to run in. The Stanford campus is large, especially given the size of the student population.

My first run at Stanford was on an old dirt track called Angel Field, at the entrance to campus in the shadow of the football stadium. I ran intervals on that track until everything hurt. Other students would sometimes try to talk to me, but I was more interested in getting my intervals done. Then I began running the campus drive loop every day: a flat run that took me through a good part of campus, past the cozy faculty houses, over to Junipero Serra Boulevard, past the golf course that I never played on, by the medical school campus, and back to my trailer. I soon discovered the run up "the dish," which was a short but steep climb up to some sort of satellite dish. It wasn't nearly as scenic or as long as the run up Mount Royal in Montreal, but it was challenging enough for a decent workout.

During my first year someone, I am not sure who, got the idea that it would be great to have a marathon-training group and run a marathon in the spring in the Northern California redwood country. It didn't take much for me to commit to that. Our group would do regular long runs together on Sunday mornings—almost always on the same route. Out Page Mill Road by Hewlett-Packard headquarters, heading west, right turn on Arastradero Road (featuring several rolling hills, at least two of which were dauntingly long and steep), another right turn once you hit Woodside Road, now heading back east towards campus. I think it was at least an eleven-mile run, although I may have slightly inflated that so I could delude myself into thinking that 26.2 would be easier with all the training. There was a time period in here where I may have been in the best shape of my life, no doubt aided by those Sunday morning runs.

Not generally a socially adept runner (and not all that socially adept, period), I nevertheless enjoyed our running group. The group normally ran at a 7:30- to 7:45-minute-per-mile pace, but I was in good enough shape that I would regularly break ahead of the pack on Arastradero Road and start ticking off seven-minute miles. Unconcerned about running protocol or etiquette, I didn't worry about whether or not someone else in the group thought I was a jerk.

For the actual race someone chose the Avenue of the Giants Marathon in Humboldt County, California. Humboldt County is right in the heart of the California redwoods, only about fifty miles south of the Oregon border. The primary industry then, and almost certainly still now, was growing weed. To get to Humboldt County from Palo Alto you cross the Golden Gate Bridge, point your car north, wind your way through the Russian River Valley, and drive for a good four or five hours.

～

I DRIVE UP BY MYSELF. Driving has always been a form of meditation for me, a bit like running, so the drive up to Humboldt the day before the race calms me down. My classmates promised me we would be staying in "rustic cabins," and even my diminished expectations are barely met. Whoever picked them out must have been specializing in cost accounting, as my wallet is much better off than the rest of me after trying to sleep in that place. I don't think I've ever slept well the night before any of my marathons, but this night is especially bad. But when I walk outside that morning into the crisp, foggy, 40-degree, ideal-marathon type of day, it's hard to be anything but hopeful. The redwoods stand firm in their majesty and my training has been my best ever.

It is cold at the start of the race, but it's a welcome-to-the-world kind of chill rather than a where-are-the-heaters type of deal. It's cold enough that I start out fast just to keep myself warm. I run between seven- and eight-minute miles the entire first half of the race without much effort. There are very few times in running when you feel like you are floating by and all parts of your body are in sync with each other and your body is in sync with the universe. This is one of them. The giant redwoods shade more than half of the course; someone close to me is yelling a loud, joyful, and primal scream every mile or two. He's either happy or crazy, or perhaps a combination of the two. This is California, after all. We run by the mile markers, with the course churning by a Northern California stream. In the early stages of a marathon, the scenery can provide a nice mental diversion; in the last six miles you don't notice it at all. I'm uncertain where my classmates are, but I'm clearly well ahead of most of them—and I couldn't be less bothered about any of that. In the end, marathoning is an individual sport. It's you, the course, the weather, your breathing, your legs, your body, and your inner will.

In every marathon I have run, there has been a point of no return. This is the point where you are either going to push through and finish, or you are going to just quit. There are two ways to quit: you can start mostly walking because it's so painful, which is a mild form of quitting; or you can literally wait for the "sag wagon," which is trolling along at a ponderous pace, picking up "sagging runners" and taking them to the finish line. The Avenue of the Giants offers me something different and—for much of the race—something I have never felt before: the sense that I can run forever.

I run the first twenty miles of the race largely on autopilot. Then the pilot light switches to the "off" position or, as they say, I hit the wall. My breath becomes labored and my legs start feeling like they have twenty-pound weights on them. Cruelly, this happens without warning. I've been tracking on not just a PR (personal record) but on demolishing my prior marathoning PR. Until I'm not anymore. The last 6.2 miles are on the other side of the point of no return. There is no way that I will quit, knowing that I could probably crawl to the finish line, but there is also no way I can keep floating along. There is a price to be paid for the delusion that you can run forever. Every marathon extracts a price. And I'm paying mine now.

Instead of cruising by mile markers, I run a tenth of a mile at a time. The most important part of pushing through the point of no return is to change your orientation towards distance. You stop thinking about the number of miles you have left, and you start "chunking up the race" into much shorter milestones. You run to the next telephone pole. You catch the runner directly in front of you, perhaps the pretty girl so that you can see what she looks like up close. You get to the next water stop. The precise nature of the game that you play doesn't matter, as long as you chunk up the race somehow. You trick your mind into thinking you are going to stop when you get to that next telephone pole, and then when you get there you trick it again. Whatever it takes to keep moving.

That's how I get through the Avenue of the Giants. The redwoods and their beauty no longer matter. Most of my classmates passing me in the last six miles don't matter either, although it is a little embarrassing. What matters is that I know I will get to the finish line, quite a bit faster than I have ever done before.

Finally, I see the finish line. It comes up suddenly. We cross one last bridge over a churning river stream. And there it is, I am done: three hours, forty-seven minutes, seventeen seconds. For real. Take that, Paul Ryan.

I don't remember much about what happens after the race, other than I do finish fast enough to take a coldish shower in the rustic cabin. Then I point the red Pontiac T-1000 back towards Palo Alto. The trip home is much calmer and more laid back than the drive up to Humboldt the day before. The Russian River Valley never looked more gorgeous. My pride in running a halfway-decent time merges with my relief that it is over, which in turn merges with the awesome beauty of Northern California. This just might be what they mean by a runner's high. I have never felt more alive.

~

TWENTY-THREE YEARS later it is 2008. I take a long weekend off work and Elaine and I go back to Humboldt. The Avenue of the Giants still exists and they are now running marathons in Humboldt twice each year, one in the spring and one in the fall. You still can't find anywhere to stay that isn't at least twenty-five miles from the start line. They are still growing lots of weed in Humboldt County.

Lots of things up here remain the same, but I am not. Running the first half of a marathon at a seven-minutes-anything pace is a distant, nostalgic memory. Was that me? Running marathons at all is becoming a memory. This time I am signed up for the half, not the full marathon. I notice something that I did not notice twenty-three years earlier. As we line up at the start, most of the other runners have about 2 percent body fat. These are the folks you can tell are marathoners even just walking down the street in jeans. I chat to a few of these guys at the start line.

The start line of a marathon can be a friendly place, even with the nervous energy vibe of the crowd. Even introverts are inclined to bare their souls when they are facing 26.2—or 13.1—miles. Even the most confident of marathoners have a little voice in their head, wondering if this is the day it will all come crashing down. It turns out that by 2008 Humboldt has a cult following. It is known for being a great training race for other, bigger marathons. Guys and women with 2 percent body fat are making the trek twice a year—religiously—to run in the redwoods, which are unchanged in their magnificence. The runners may take notice of the redwoods, but nature is not recip-rocal. The redwoods could care less about the runners, who come and go as the redwoods stand their ground.

4

MASSEY FRIENDLY VOYAGEUR MARATHON

M
assey, Ontario, July 1992, 4 hours, 14 minutes

"Tell me, what is it you plan to do with your one wild and precious life?"
Mary Oliver

THE DAY before I graduated from Stanford in 1986, Elaine and I married in Cincinnati. It was a small wedding in the chapel of the church where she and I met. After the reception at her house on Erie Avenue, we flew to San Jose to make my graduation day and move my stuff out of my grad student apartment in Palo Alto. I insisted on putting all of my articles from business school into organized binders, which after stuffing them into my Pontiac T-1000, we did together while we were in Mendocino on our honeymoon. I suspect Elaine had something to say about spending part of her honeymoon punching three holes into business school articles and putting them into binders, reflecting her lack of enthusiasm for this activity. That lack of enthusiasm was further reinforced when the binders sat unloved in our attic, creating a fire hazard. It took me twenty years to admit the error of my ways and throw them out. The rest of our honeymoon consisted of driving back across country to Cincinnati, but at least she got to see Mount Rushmore along the way.

My first job after business school was with a healthcare software start-up in a suburb of Detroit that was intending to revolutionize healthcare delivery with new technology capturing patient data at the hospital bedside. I was definitely drinking the healthcare tech Kool-Aid at that point; over thirty years later the software guys are still trying to revolutionize healthcare delivery, investors are still investing in that potential, and the healthcare industry moves on relatively untouched by it all. Sometime during those thirty years I've learned that changing what doctors and patients do isn't so easy.

My stepson, Rik, came with us to Detroit, so the three of us went looking for a house to rent together. We found a great place in a northern suburb: a spacious ranch-style house with an adjoining pond, and Rik and I loved the place. But when we turned to ask Elaine what she thought, she was crying. I took this as a cue that she didn't like the place. Something about way too many mosquitos next to the pond and the house being more than a little dirty. I guess we picked the wrong time of day to show her this gem of a house; maybe we should have waited until it was dark out. Anyway, we ended up renting a more traditional ranch-style property in a nice neighborhood of a nice suburb, which soon enough all three of us started to hate.

Elaine's ex-husband, the aggressive lawyer in Chicago, decided shortly after we got married to file for custody of Rik. We spent the next year enmeshed in the case. I should pause here to note that Elaine was and is a wonderfully fantastic mother: supportive, loving, caring, tolerant, giving, easy to talk to. Everyone from teachers to psychologists testified on her behalf, but the case was tried in the Chicago suburbs and her ex didn't face any legal costs since he was represented by someone who worked for him. We ended up losing

custody in a decision that was delayed three months without explanation, leaving us to speculate the rest of our lives if something shady
(like money in the judge's pocket) might have swayed the ruling.

Both Elaine and I were devastated by the decision. We went out
for pizza that night but we were in such a daze that I couldn't even
taste the pepperoni. We will never know exactly why we lost custody
and that's the kind of thing that can drive you crazy if you let it.
Elaine's whole life revolved around being a mom and losing daily
access to her ten-year-old son—even phone calls—was heartbreak-
ing. Maybe something shady did happen, but there were also signs
that the judge was impressed with Elaine's ex being a lawyer making
a lot of money. And I was a guy one year out of business school with
no money and some student debt.

Elaine had a much more productive and mature reaction to this
devastating life event than I did, since she always kept her focus on
Rik and worked hard to keep being his mom. Meanwhile, I was
pissed off about the whole thing, including the part where the case
was drawn out for eleven months and Elaine had to travel back and
forth to Chicago many times. But I did understand on a deep gut-
level a few things that turned out to be helpful in the longer run.
Most importantly, I knew that Rik needed to live with his dad for a
while to sort out his childhood.

So, the best thing to do was just put one foot in front of the other
and carry on. There are some things that happen to you in life that
you can't ever totally get over, but you can choose to go on living. And
time does work in your favor, giving you more perspective and even
hope if you can just keep going. A lot like running a marathon,
actually.

We both needed a change in scenery and, after a promising start,
I wasn't all that happy in my job after all. So, we made a quick decision to move back to Cincinnati, the place where Elaine and I had
met and considered home. Basically, we needed something positive to
happen and moving back to Cincinnati was what we could come up
with. To us, Cincinnati had soul, the kind of soul that you don't get
for free but only through your own living history. Over time, it

worked. We lived in a beautiful, large second-floor apartment with a big front porch sitting over Madison Road on the east side of Cincinnati, in Hyde Park. I still drive by that apartment occasionally, and think about that tumultuous time in our lives.

Predictably, Rik living with his dad, and equally significantly his dad's crazy girlfriend, was initially an unmitigated disaster. Six months in, they sent him to a Catholic military school in the middle of Indiana. This was probably for the best, since the girlfriend turned out to be a cocaine addict, in addition to being generally unbalanced. It's unbelievable how clueless Elaine and I were about the signs; Rik used to call us from their summer vacation home and say, "Hey, she stays up all night and sleeps during the day and blows her nose all the time." We still didn't connect the dots. It was only when Rik told us when he was fourteen that his dad was driving him across Austin Avenue in Chicago to buy drugs, basically clobbering us over the head with the hard facts, that we realized she was an addict.

Within a few years after that, his dad had married and divorced again, and Rik was moved to a new junior high school where he once again lived on campus. In high school, Rik spent less and less time with his dad and new wife, and more time microwaving his own dinners. Pretty soon he was spending every summer, nearly every holiday, and many weekends with us. And along the way Rik did, to his everlasting credit—especially when he got out of Chicago after he graduated from high school—develop an honest and constructive relationship with his father.

I dealt with the custody case and surrounding drama in my usual way: I ran. Especially when I returned to my neighborhood in Hyde Park, home of wide streets, tons of runners of all ages, and several familiar running routes. I got a job that was slightly more normal, although that didn't mean that I myself was normal—I was still intense about work and not so good at life balance. But my running was now rounding off the edges of my life, rather than being an obsession that added more edge.

Some of this had to do with Elaine. Unlike my first wife, she liked that I ran. In fact, once she discovered that I was almost always in a better mood afterwards, she began suggesting it: "Hey, Dougy, why don't you go out for a run and then we can talk about this big issue after you get back?" More often than not, the big issue that we were talking about before I went running was no longer an issue by the time I came home. We didn't even need to talk at all. The body can work in miraculous ways.

When it came to running, a pattern was emerging. I would "quit" running marathons "for good" and then, after I forgot how painful marathons were towards the end, I would try to run another one. It was like some kind of perverse addiction, except what I was addicted to was good for me.

We spent the next four years in Cincinnati where I mostly focused on my job, but the whole time I was working my way back to running long distances without admitting it to anyone, especially myself. I got in the habit of driving out to Loveland, about twenty-five minutes from home, to run on a bike trail. The rumor was that the trail went all the way up north to Springfield about seventy miles away, but I never verified that. I would have if I'd still had my ten-speed bike. But I used the drive up to the trail to think about my run and the drive back to recover from my run, and soon I was doing runs ten miles or longer once a week. By the summer of 1992, I had the marathon-running bug again. And when I catch that bug, I can do some stupid things.

Like trying to find a marathon to run in the middle of July when 85 degrees is considered mild in Cincinnati. In a burst of rational thought, I decided that I would probably need to head north to pull off a marathon. The only one that I could find was in a little town called Massey, 225 miles east of Sault Sainte Marie, Ontario. In other words, smack-dab in the middle of nowhere. I had been to Sault Sainte Marie before when I was a kid and I didn't remember it as much of anything. But heading for Massey, Ontario, in the middle of July was no big deal to me, since I never had any problem with driving long distances. Heck, when I went to Stanford, I made four cross-country trips—three of them by myself and one with Elaine right after I graduated for our "honeymoon." Driving long distances was, to me, another form of meditation, much like running except without all of the effort and calorie burning.

I knew Elaine probably wasn't up for a driving weekend that ended up in Massey, Ontario, which I figured—correctly, as it turned out—was not exactly a major tourist destination. So, I asked a guy at work whom I didn't know too well—but who was single and just getting into running—if he wanted to make the trip with me. He said yes. Then I asked Elaine if she was okay with me spending three or four days on this rather strange adventure, and miraculously she said she was. I suspect there might have been some serious eye-rolling when I asked her, but I don't remember. Elaine was setting new standards for tolerating my crazy ideas, something that would be put to the test many more times in the future.

Following this impeccable logic, I found myself in the heat of the summer of 1992 packing for a trip to Massey, Ontario, wherever that was. Just about the same time that a young-looking politician on TV named Bill Clinton, from some remote place in Arkansas, was accepting the Democratic Party nomination to run for president. It all felt very hopeful—maybe I could run a decent marathon in the middle of July after all, and maybe I could finally vote for a president who actually won the election.

∼

GETTING to Massey turns out to be most of the fun, but, then again, we are talking about "fun" relative to running a marathon in the middle of July. My new friend Rob and I drive north up into Michigan, cut into Ontario at Port Huron, make a scenic drive up the southern coast of Lake Huron, and then take a ferry across Lake Huron to Manitoulin Island, which I had never heard of until this trip. Our aim is to get to Massey in time to receive our race numbers and have the pre-race pasta meal (spaghetti); for some reason that bad Italian meal was important to both of us. Even in our haste I take note that Manitoulin Island is splendidly remote and mostly untouched by humanoids, except for a few charming villages. We get to Massey about as fast as possible when you have to factor two ferry rides into your trip—one to get onto Manitoulin Island and one to get off.

Massey meets my expectations, which are approximately zero. It isn't much, beyond a few motels, some gas stations, a school where the race starts and ends, and a small town. It also isn't much cooler than it had been in Cincinnati when we left, the only difference being that the crazy Canadians are up for hosting a mid-July marathon. Our motel room is average even by Massey standards, but we're reducing marathon running down to the bare fundamentals anyway. What else do you need besides running shorts, running shoes, a bunch of Gatorade, the barely edible pre-race pasta, and a motel room where you can sleep fitfully since you're worried about the race?

We wake up to a sunny Ontario morning hotter than it should be in Canada in July, a bad cup of coffee, and a start line. Whatever the polar opposite is of a "big city marathon," the Massey Marathon is that. Still, all of the basics are in place, even the essential port-o-lets. And the saving grace is that Canadians are, as everyone knows, much nicer than Americans. Much, much nicer. When you throw together Canadian-nice with small-town-nice, Massey is an incredibly nice place to find ourselves.

There aren't too many other folks who have made this trek to Massey on July 19, 1992. The thing about marathons like this in remote places is that they tend to attract hard-core runners—people whose concept of fun is driving something like five hundred miles to run a marathon in a small town in the middle of nowhere in July—and then a few local stragglers who have somehow stumbled onto the idea of trying to run 26.2 miles for the first time. The only difference in Massey is that they are marking things off in kilometers rather than miles. This is actually great since you hit more kilometer markers than mile markers, creating the welcome delusion of progress. It gets progressively harder to do the metric conversion in my head the further I run, but I know that when I get to forty kilometers I am almost done, and when I get to forty-two, I am pretty much completely done.

There is a small problem. I haven't exactly trained to run a marathon; whether you measure it in miles or kilometers, it is longer than my body is prepared to run. I start out at an even pace, which I hold through the first twenty miles or so. But then I start to fade. It isn't a total crash/flame-out, a calamity that I will soon learn I am also capable of. Neither is it a slow marathon shuffle, where your brain tells you that you are running and consequently you think you are running—but no one watching you actually knows you are running and your watch eventually confirms that. But it is a definite fade. I run most of the rest of the race at that slow-fade pace with some walking through the water stops involved in the enterprise. I try to break four hours, but just cannot hold on. I end up crossing the finish line in four hours and fourteen minutes and a now unknown number of seconds, still redeemed by the fact that I finish well ahead of Rob. I'm bummed out that I don't break four hours, and seriously dehydrated, but the Canadians are nice to me at the finish. Very nice.

We drive home via Manitoulin Island, which, after all, is the only way to get there. We stay on the island that first night after the day of the marathon. The place has the kind of natural beauty that's only possible if you don't have too many people hanging around, the year-round population being only around 12,000. It is gorgeous, the only problem being that I'm with this guy I hardly know rather than Elaine. Canada still seems like the great undiscovered land to me. Being attracted to driving, I've always had a fantasy of just taking off for Alaska and driving right up through the Northwest Territories, but I've never actually pulled that one off.

~

ELAINE'S TOLERANCE for my Massey Marathon adventure was stunning. When I got home she just wanted to hear about the whole trip; there didn't seem to be any questioning of the rationale in heading up to Canada to run a marathon on July 19. I'm no expert on relationships but I took this as a good sign. When I was at Stanford and she was in Cincinnati, at times it didn't seem like we were getting along too well. We had the primary problem of the distance between us and the secondary problem of not having much money. Plus, we both had a fair amount of stress in our lives, with hers being greater than mine. I had the stress of figuring out how to get through Stanford business school and then figuring out what to do after I graduated. But she had the stress of making a living, of which she did a fine job, while simultaneously raising Rik with her ex-husband in the background, creating problems at every opportunity. And raising Rik was like raising more than just one kid: nothing was simple. Between all that stress, we had many long and difficult phone calls.

Chance and luck have worked in my favor when it comes to my relationship with Elaine. I think it starts with the fact that we share the same values, even though we are incredibly different people. We care about the same stuff, including each other. We are tolerant of each other, even in situations where other couples might not be, and part of what we value is "not telling the other person what to do." Which is important because we are both independent and stubborn. Actually, she's independent and I'm stubborn.

Right around the summer of 1992, when the Massey Marathon adventure was happening, our relationship found a new, positive cadence. We both loved being back in Cincinnati. It's just a place that feeds our souls. We liked the grittiness of city life and we found a nice house with enough room for the two of us, and close to everything anyone could possibly ever need—coffee, yogurt, running paths, and Whole Foods. We had that ever-elusive sense that we were "home."

Things were not perfect, of course. For one thing, I was working too much. I had started working again at the same small software company in Cincinnati that I worked at before Stanford. The sense that it was a backwards step professionally was mitigated by the fact that they were the only folks willing to bet on me, with no marketing experience, as their marketing director. They might have just been desperate.

The place was full of crazy characters, some of whom were downright weird. Software development was even more of a black art then than it is now, and even now it is hardly a science. The first software developer I met when I walked in was some 350-pound guy named Jason, and the first thing he asked me was if I was part of Mensa. I have steered clear of Mensa ever since. Most small software companies cannot pass the "one truck test" where they can afford to lose any of their software developers, and we were certainly no exception to this. Software developers aren't dumb, certainly not about their own importance, so it's easy to end up with "the inmates running the asylum," like some real-life version of *One Flew Over the Cuckoo's Nest.* We spent a lot of time trying to deal with keeping the software developers happy and never cracked the code on that. Other than buying them free food.

We actually had some good products that did interesting things for our customers, like storing and managing all the engineering drawings for an aerospace company, all the personnel records for large military bases, and all the aircraft registration records for the Federal Aviation Administration. I still can't believe they trusted us with all that stuff. And I was responsible for new product innovation, which was a cool job, perhaps in part because I didn't know what I was doing. A disgruntled sales guy told me about his idea to build a product that not only retrieved all this documentation but also managed the whole change control cycle for approving new document revisions. I took his idea and decided to make it a reality. Which eventually took me back to the lovable but weird software developers.

It was a heady time, at least for me, but I had no idea how to balance work with the rest of my life. I worked a lot of hours, but even worse, when I was not "working" I was still thinking about work all the time. This wasn't a great way to live to be sure. Mark Twain once said, "I've lived through some terrible things in my life, some of which actually happened." That was unfortunately how I seemed to relate to my work back then.

5
_____

NEW YORK CITY MARATHON

N*ew York City, November 1992, 4 hours, 37 minutes*

"The city seen from the Queensboro Bridge is always the city seen for the first time, in its first wild promise of all the mystery and beauty in the world."
F. Scott Fitzgerald

AT LAST, we managed to save a bit of money from my five years of work in Cincinnati. We weren't making a ton of money but Cincinnati was a relatively cheap place to live. It was time for a new car, my red Pontiac T-1000 that had gotten me to California and back twice having finally bitten the dust. Elaine and Rik and I went to a Mazda dealer in Cincinnati.

By then Rik was about fifteen and he had figured out that I wasn't the best negotiator in the world. I hate spending a lot of time shopping, even for big things like cars. Unfortunately, just as the sales-person came up to us, Elaine went into the restroom. Rik was terrified I would actually buy a car before she got out. As I began talking to the salesperson, he started banging on the restroom door, yelling, "Mom, Mom. You need to come out. Doug is starting to talk to the salesperson."

Once Elaine imposed some order and rationality (and negotiating skills) on the situation, we ended up buying a blue Mazda 323 for a little over nine grand. It was a great car that eventually lasted over ten years and 200,000 miles. It became a game of mine to see how many miles I could put on it before it went to the junkyard. The car and I got along well, each of us adapting to the other's personality. I had problems back then maintaining a good posture, in part because I hadn't started cross-training or lifting light weights yet. After a while, whenever I leaned forward too much the seatbelt buzzer would go off, even though I had my seatbelt on. When I straightened out my posture, the damn thing would finally shut up.

A year or so later, one morning I was headed for the coffee shop and my driver's-side door got stuck on the high curb. I yanked on the door with the handle in an effort to shut it. The entire driver's side handle ended up in my hand, completely unattached. Fortunately, there was another way to shut the door, so I just threw the handle on the floor behind the passenger seat, where it stayed for another five or six years. Neither the car nor I seemed too bothered about it.

The Mazda 323 also was a dead giveaway to many folks about my true personality. One of the guys who worked for me later on told me that as soon as he saw the car he knew I was an okay guy. I've read lots of books my whole life and at one point I began storing my books in the backseat. One of my co-workers, who would ride in the back-seat when more than two of us went out to lunch, said it was like having a library at hand.

Eventually, after the Mazda clocked up over 200K miles, Elaine volunteered to trade cars with me. I thought that was strange since her car was much nicer than mine. The next thing I knew, my Mazda was parked on our street for three months unable to start, and soon after that someone called the cops and it got hauled away to the junk-yard. I noticed that Elaine wasn't too unhappy about its demise.

Soon after I got the Mazda I came up with what I thought was a brilliant idea. Elaine had never seen New York City and I was wanting to atone for my disappointing finish in the Massey Marathon. One day I said to her, "Hey, why don't I run the New York City Marathon in November and we can drive to New York?" That seemed okay with Elaine. This was back when NYC was an easier marathon to get into; there was some kind of lottery system but most applicants were able to get into the race. I booked a room at the Embassy Suites on Times Square—which was no problem, since the marathon was not as over-booked back then and Times Square was a drug-infested dump rather than the cleaned-up version of Disney World that it is now.

One day in late fall 1992 we pointed the blue Mazda east and took off driving. The ten-hour drive was uneventful until we crossed the George Washington Bridge into Manhattan. At that point about five young, rough-looking guys descended upon our Mazda while it was parked at a red light to give us a "car wash." It wasn't a voluntary car wash. After I dug enough money out of my wallet to get them to move out of the way, we were on our way into the heart of Manhattan. Welcome to New York City, the Ohio license plates likely being an important trigger for our involuntary car wash. I've driven all over the United States, but trying to find the Embassy Suites and a place to park the car in the middle of rush hour traffic was truly terrifying. The dark feeling in the pit of my stomach stayed with me all through Manhattan, and I haven't driven there since.

Despite this trauma, I was excited for Elaine to see New York City for the first time. As soon as we checked into the Embassy Suites, we went out to a modest Italian restaurant a few blocks away. After dinner Elaine started getting nauseated and she proceeded to remain in bed the entire weekend of the marathon. So much for showing her New York City. It was a definite blessing that the suites in Embassy Suites had two rooms. I went off to pick up my race number, which was the point at which it actually dawned on me that there were an awful lot of people running the marathon that weekend.

The problem with "big city marathons," I was about to learn first-hand, is that they are logistical nightmares. If you want to find your spouse or significant other, or just cruise up to the start line without much thought, run a smaller marathon. On the other hand, big city marathons do have a few advantages. There is a decent chance the sheer size of the spectacle will get your adrenaline pumping in the most positive way. Or, if it doesn't, perhaps your pulse rate is too low. Also, in a big city marathon you don't need to worry about the embarrassment of finishing last. I can guarantee you there will be someone slower than you.

Running New York City just might be the biggest logistical challenge of all. First, you need to catch one of the buses for runners to get from Manhattan to Staten Island. I caught mine at the downtown library with the Sunday *New York Times* in hand. I turned to the sports page and decided to read up on, what else? The New York City Marathon. I figured this would keep me occupied on the bus ride where I didn't know anyone and everyone else looked as stressed out as I did about running the marathon. There was a column of particular interest to me called "Mistakes Not to Make If You Are Running New York for the First Time," or some such thing. I read it with intense interest. The writer particularly emphasized being careful on the Verrazano Bridge, the one connecting Staten Island to Brooklyn at the start of the race. The bridge is heavily sloped, and when the adrenaline is pumping at the start of the race it's easy to run the second mile of the race, which is mostly on the downslope of the Verrazano Bridge, too fast. At least according to the *New York Times*.

～

ONCE WE ARRIVE at Staten Island, they put us into big tents. We have about three hours to kill before the start of the race. Plenty of time for a few stops at the port-o-lets, at least. The problem is that it is the coldest day in the history of the New York City Marathon, in the mid-thirties at the start of the race. Staying loose is nearly impossible, since I am freezing as I wait. Many of the runners deal with this situation by doing what runners do: running. This might keep them warmer, but I can't see the point. Given that I'm about to run (well, hopefully run) 26.2 miles, why would I run a couple of miles before the start of the actual race? So, I mostly just hang around and stretch with the occasional semi-polite conversations with other runners thrown in.

Finally, after three hours of sitting and standing in the cold, the gun goes off. This is only semi-relevant to me, as even though I have been standing at the starting line freezing for about forty-five minutes beforehand, the marathon hosts 25,000 runners or so, and it is ten minutes after the "start" that I actually begin running. There is plenty of hoopla—balloons, tugboats in the river below blaring their horns. Everyone seems freaking happy for a group about to run 26.2 miles in the freezing cold.

I try to get into meditation mode to calm down, muttering to myself "breathe deep" under my breath a few times. But it's hard not to get caught up in the hoopla. I half-run/half-walk the first mile up the Verrazano Bridge. There are so many other runners I'm trying hard not to trip over someone else, and certainly it is my objective to not fall off the bridge itself. By the time I crest the top and hit the downslope, I am totally pumped up, especially since I'm actually starting to warm up. My stride feels great, my breathing is now naturally deep, and I finally have enough room to actually run.

I pick up my pace but it doesn't seem like a big deal. I notice that I might be running a little too fast down that bridge. And—very stupidly—it turns out that I actually am. I run the second mile, down the Verrazano Bridge, in six minutes and eighteen seconds—a ridiculously fast pace given that even a great marathon pace for me would be about eight minutes and thirty seconds.

So much for taking advice from the *New York Times*. Somewhere in the back of my mind it occurs to me that I have made the exact bonehead move—the "first-timer's mistake"—that I was reading about a few hours before on the bus. But I feel great, so maybe—hopefully—I just picked up a few minutes. Maybe I've just "burned off" nervous energy, I try to reassure myself. I push the thought that I might have already blown my one-and-only New York City Marathon into the deep recesses of my mind.

I settle into a much slower pace as we wind through Brooklyn, headed for Queens, and then I notice something else. As we run in the boroughs, the sun comes out, increasing the temperature. But then every time we get on one of those bridges high above the water, with nothing to break the wind, I am freezing again. In every other marathon I have run, I could just layer my clothing and everything was fine. Usually I would just wear an old ratty long-sleeve T-shirt as the outer layer, so that I could throw it into a trash can (or hang it on a tree limb) when I got too hot. But today is different, as my body switches from cold to hot and back to cold—over and over again.

I hang in there at a decent pace—about eight-and-a-half-minute miles—through the first half of the race. To the extent that I can notice anything other than myself and my breathing and my stride, it is an amazing scene. There are crowds three-deep nearly the whole race, cheering loudly for friends or maybe just for all of us runners in general. Not being an experienced New Yorker, I am seeing all five boroughs for the first time in the best possible way. At least, right then at about mile thirteen, it seemed like the best possible way.

At the halfway mark, which is the Pulaski Bridge that connects Brooklyn and Queens, I'm still feeling pretty decent. But there's that nagging feeling, fueled by my inability to process the pre-race advice from the *New York Times*, that it might all fall apart. Around the sixteen-mile mark, I arrive at the Queensboro Bridge (also known as the 59th Street Bridge), which takes you into Manhattan. I climb the steep hill to get onto the bridge; the wind is howling and I'm on an icy grated bridge. I try to look straight in front of me rather than down through the grates into the river. This proves a challenge.

Coming off the Queensboro Bridge, I get my reward. I run onto First Avenue in Manhattan to the biggest roar I have ever heard in my life, certainly for anything remotely athletic that I am part of. If there is a bigger thrill for a below-average runner like me than this kind of roar, I don't know what it is. I engage in the delusion that everyone is cheering for me alone, my mind just off-kilter enough after sixteen miles of hard running that I almost believe it. I'm not going to stop or slow down now. I can't even hear myself breathe the whole way down First Avenue.

I am cruising now. And then two and a half miles later, I crash. I'm in an ugly part of the Bronx and I crash ugly. Every muscle in my body tightens up in the space of five minutes or so. Everything hurts. I am struggling big-time just to keep running. I think back to that crazy 6:18 mile coming down off the Verrazano Bridge at the start. What an idiot I am. It's all coming back to haunt me. I go into shuffle mode and it's obvious that my New York City Marathon is effectively over. But there is no way I am going to quit, or wait around for the sag wagon. So, I shuffle some more, then walk some more, then shuffle some more, for the next eight miles. I cross into Central Park, thinking that I am getting close to the finish line, forgetting it's a big place. Spectators are drinking beer and yelling out my race number and telling me to start running. I'm reminded that, runner cama- raderie aside, I am in New York after all.

I continue my marathon shuffle/walk through the three or four miles of Central Park, which, by the way, is very hilly for a city park. Finally, I see the finish line in the distance. I cross it in four hours and thirty-seven minutes, anticlimactically. Whatever sun the day brought is now totally gone and I am freezing again. I remember that Elaine is still back at the Embassy Suites, lying in bed, sick. I don't quite know how to get back to the hotel, but it's clear that I am going to have to walk it, no matter how far I've already gone or how cold I am. There are no cabs in sight. I finally find the hotel. Sheepishly, we head out of town and stick New York City in the rearview mirror, as fast as we can. As soon as we hit Pennsylvania, Elaine feels good again. She must have been allergic to New York City.

My participation aside, the 1992 New York City Marathon is notable for two reasons. First, it remains to this day the coldest one on record. And second, the race founder and director, Fred Lebow, ran the entire race with the famed Norwegian female marathoner, Grete Waitz. Fred had brain cancer and Grete ran at his pace. They finished together, holding hands, in 5:32. A few months after that,

Fred died. Tragically, Grete herself later died in 2011, at age fifty-seven, of breast cancer.

⤳

BACK IN CINCINNATI, I was glad to be finished with New York and I had no desire to go back and run another big city marathon anytime soon. My marathons were beginning to cluster themselves into two categories. In the first, and unfortunately more common category, were the marathons where I would crash somewhere between the eighteen and twenty-two-mile mark, and then walk/shuffle my way to the finish line. I seemed to have enough will, or maybe just enough stubbornness, to keep going to the finish line. But these marathons were painful and even a little bit embarrassing, especially when I crashed closer to the eighteen-mile mark, like I did in New York. In all of these cases, I went out too fast at the start and couldn't seem to manage my over-hyped adrenaline at the beginning of the race. I felt great for the first ten miles or so, having no clue that I was headed for the infamous "wall." It was like the logical part of my brain was over-taken by adrenaline and emotion, or maybe just plan stupidity. Even when my watch told me I was going too fast I kept going too fast—until I started to tighten up and then it was too late. Then I'd usually run okay for another three or four miles until I crashed. I didn't seem to have the ability to "save" the run by recovering during the race.

The other category of marathons went much better. I would start out slow, so slow that after five miles I would have hardly broken a sweat. Then I'd start to gradually pick up my pace, just a few seconds per mile at a time. By the time I'd get to the twenty-mile mark, I knew with some degree of confidence—although nowhere near total certainty—that I had enough gas in the tank to finish. It was a good feeling. Especially when I'd pass people after the twenty-mile mark, gliding past them smoothly and quietly and usually without saying a word.

In the running world, there is the concept of running "negative splits," which means that you run the second half of the race—

however long the race is—faster than the first half. It is a glorious concept. And one that I have rarely been able to put into practice. When you run negative splits, you feel great at the end. You finish strong, look good at the finish line, and recover much easier than when you hit the wall.

Elaine, of course, had all this figured out. Before every race she'd say to me, "Now, Dougy, make sure you go out slow." I'd nod my head as if I was hearing every word. And then, normally, I'd proceed to ignore her advice, go out too fast, and hit the wall anyway. And whine about it to her after the race, ignoring the fact that I had ignored her advice. I haven't had any genetic testing done but if I ever do, I am sure they will find "the stubborn gene."

Meanwhile, life was good back in Cincinnati but work wasn't that great. I had a good job at the small tech company but my work was beginning to feel like the *Groundhog Day* movie, with every year looking too much like the one before it. There was no real chance to move up, since my boss was the CEO. One day, I got a call from a recruiter at Heidrick & Struggles about a job with one of our larger competitors up in Ann Arbor. I agreed to a meeting with the recruiter, who flew into the Cincinnati airport to meet me in one of those frequent flyer clubs. Gretchen was tall and personable, and about to get married to an airline pilot. She was also pitching hard a job as vice president of marketing and product management in a small tech company that paid a lot more than my current position. I agreed to take the next step and meet with the CEO and the woman who was running HR.

A few weeks later, Elaine and I had dinner with the two of them at an old, now long-gone steakhouse in downtown Cincinnati named La Normandie. I liked them and I felt ready for a new challenge. I agreed to go up to Ann Arbor and learn more about the place. On Memorial Day weekend, Elaine and I drove up and I met with my British predecessor, who was going to stay with the company in a different job. He was arrogant, and seemed to know just about everything except how to do the job he was supposed to be doing.

Soon all sorts of red flags were waving beyond the arrogant

British guy, including and especially the fact that no one respected or got along with the CEO, known here as "George." I've always been good at saying just about anything to anybody—being direct in an understated way helps with this—so I spoke to George before I took the job and shared with him that he seemed to be part of the problem. He reassured me that he would change. But, of course, in the end he didn't. My belief in George turned out to be only mistake number one: I hadn't yet learned that people can want to change but still find it impossible to do so. And the job did pay about 50 percent more than I was earning in Cincinnati, which seemed like a good reason to take it. And that turned out to be mistake number two.

6

COLUMBUS MARATHON

C olumbus, Ohio, October 1993, 3 hours, 54 minutes

"The greatest glory in living lies not in never falling but in rising every time you fall."
Nelson Mandela

I DECIDED to run the Columbus Marathon in the Fall of 1993. In comparison with previous races, this would be logistically easy, since Elaine and I owned the condo in northwest Columbus that my parents lived in. Furthermore, the course would be flat and conducive to a fast time. It bugged me that I had faded so badly the past November in New York City. I wanted to cleanse my system, and history, of that bad race.

On marathon race day my dad drove me down to the course; this was before he started getting Alzheimer's disease and when he could still drive. The game plan was for Dad to drop me off and Elaine to come pick me up at the finish line—hopefully not literally. I knew that my dad was somewhat proud of me, even though he never actually expressed much interest or curiosity about what I was doing with my life. As we were driving down to the race he asked me how far the marathon was.

"It's 26.2 miles, Dad." I looked over at him as he processed that for a while.

"Wow," he said suddenly. 'That's longer than the drive between Bowling Green and Toledo. That's a long way. I can't believe you can run that far." His eyes were big.

I was taken aback. This was one of the few times in my life that my father had openly expressed amazement at something I was doing. The Bowling Green-to-Toledo comparison had reduced it down to something he could wrap his brain around. What he said, and especially the way he said it, gave me enough confidence that I pushed into the back of my mind the question of whether or not I actually could still run 26.2 miles.

~

THE MARATHON STARTS OUT DOWNTOWN, but is soon running by The Ohio State University. The course heads north up High Street and then winds to the west around Upper Arlington. As we head up High Street, a couple of guys banter about the home run that Joe Carter hit the night before to win the 1993 World Series for the Toronto Blue Jays. That's how I find out the Blue Jays had won; I've always had a knack for eavesdropping.

After it lands back downtown, the course continues east into Bexley, close to where my friend Dave lives. I would have told him that I was running that day, but I didn't want to create any expectations. It's enough pressure to actually run the marathon, let alone have someone waiting for me on the course and asking me exactly when I expect to be there. Especially in the twenty-two-mile marker range—how the heck could I know?

The marathon is going well except for one little problem. There is almost always one little problem in marathon running. You can train all you want for any marathon, but you never know what you are going to experience until you actually get there. I had noticed a slight tightness high in my left groin area while doing my training. Around mile eighteen, the tightness becomes suddenly more pronounced. At mile marker twenty, I spy a small building with an empty parking lot to my left. Perfect. I stop and stretch my left leg and groin area as I lean on the building. I hardly ever stop to stretch in the middle of any race but the tightness is starting to bother me. The pain is noticeable and it's disconcerting to not know the source of it.

After about thirty seconds of stretching, I return to the course, having decided the pain is bearable. My goal is to finish the race in under four hours, and I know that is well with my grasp. Other than this strange tightness that is changing my stride, my legs feel good and my breathing is normal. Somewhere around mile twenty-two in Bexley, I know that I will break four hours. In the last few miles the course heads through Columbus's version of a hip urban district, German Village, and then finishes downtown. The fall day is cool enough to make marathon running seem sane, and the crowds are much thicker at the finish line than anywhere else on the course. I cross the finish line in three hours and fifty-four minutes, beating four hours with more than five minutes to spare.

Afterwards I'm happy, but I'm not exactly walking too well. Due to my groin tightness, my stride became funky late in the race—even though my pace didn't slow too much. I whine a little to Elaine but she mostly ignores me. It isn't that she lacks empathy—she's great at empathy—she just also knows that I am a hypochondriac and that if you ignore most of my whining, it goes away after a few days.

When we get back to Ann Arbor, where I was working by then, I begin stretching out my groin harder and harder. This turns out not to be one of my smartest decisions. Most runners think you can get hurt running marathons, which is true, but in my experience the riskiest time is actually the few days after the marathon. Marathon runners being, for the most part, fanatics of the first order, always want to get back into training prematurely. The one thing a real runner hates the most is being idle. But your body has a cadence of its own, which you choose to ignore at your peril. I am about to learn this the hard way. My left groin gets progressively worse, and every time I try to run fast I feel a knot down there. I can't generate any push off my left leg, so I can't generate any speed. Not that I've ever been a speed demon, but this is getting bad.

All of this lands me a trip to the University of Michigan Sports Medicine Clinic, which sounds like a cool place—and it is a cool place, right up until the moment a young doctor informs me I have a torn adductor muscle in my left groin. My "therapy" is to receive regular ultrasound from a physical therapist and to lay off running hard for about six months.

Stopping running temporarily may sound like a relatively trivial health problem—since in fact, it is a relatively trivial health problem —but I managed to impose the maximum amount of drama into the situation, nearly all of which I took out on Elaine. How could I *not* train hard for six months? How was I going to manage the stress of my increasingly stressful job without being able to run? How could anyone know how long the recovery time would be? What if the sports medicine guys were wrong about what was wrong with my leg? There were so many questions, and no answers that could calm my monkey mind.

In truth, I didn't mind all the drama, which included me talking incessantly to Elaine about how hard it would be to not run for six months, as well as going to physical therapy three times a week to get ultrasound on the torn muscle. In fact, I rather liked all the attention. It was kind of like when I was in high school and I was hoping that there was some way I could break my arm, so that all the girls I wanted to date would come up and sign my cast. Which never happened.

What I did mind was that I could not actually run for six months, at least not hard. I spent a bunch of time doing a stretching exercise where I had to lie on the floor right next to a wall and then put my legs up on the wall and stretch them as wide as I could. This worked well until Elaine discovered my shoes were making marks all over the wall.

The physical therapists at U-M Sports Medicine Clinic recommended that I work out on the indoor track by the tennis courts at the U-M athletic complex. It was a fine track—I think it was a quarter-mile one. The problem was that I couldn't run a full lap around it at anywhere near full speed. Elaine told me to stop being obsessive about my problems, something that can work only if you can catch me in a moment of temporary self-insight. She finally caught me in one of those moments.

Up until then, I'd been lucky when it came to running injuries, and I've been lucky ever since. I seem to run without much bounce and thus do not put undue stress on my knees or other joints. My most frequent problem has been falling down, usually the result of some external object—like, for example, a dog—that gets in my way. About a year ago I was running down a sidewalk next to a road when I came up on a guy walking his dog. I failed to say "passing on the left" as I went past them and the dog turned out to be a little pit bull in training. I learned quickly why runners say "passing on the left" when they pass someone on the left. As luck would have it, when the pit bull leapt at me I happened to be in one of the few stretches on that road where there was a curb between the sidewalk and the street. As I jerked to my left to avoid getting mauled, my left foot hit the curb and I flew onto the street hands first, with my Gatorade bottle careening down the street about twenty-five yards ahead of me. The guy walking his dog asked me if I was okay before I had a chance to collect myself and get up. Not wanting to cause a scene (which was ludicrous, since I already had), I immediately said yes, before I knew if I was okay or not. It turned out the guy was a mail carrier on vacation, so he had plenty of sympathy for getting leapt at by a dog, and perhaps, now that I think of it, that's why he wanted his own pit bull. But this was no time to psychoanalyze him. Once I collected myself and started running again I discovered I actually was okay, other than a bloody knee and a few scrapes on my hand. My ribs were a little sore, but the next week I managed to drive over a thousand miles and run a decent half marathon.

My most infamous fall, though, was one beautiful October day in Cincinnati when I was twelve miles into a thirteen-miler. It was a calm Sunday, at least until I fell, and I was feeling great. I had run all the way from Hyde Park to Eden Park and back, about twelve miles total, and as I came back through Hyde Park Square I noticed two middle-aged guys walking down the sidewalk holding hands. This diverted my attention at precisely the wrong moment. As I fixated my gaze on them while coming up from behind, I failed to notice both the rake leaning against some steps next to the sidewalk and a major-league crack in the sidewalk. Either the rake or the sidewalk itself, I never figured out which, took my legs out from under me just as I was passing the two guys holding hands. I landed on my face, and when I looked up my glasses were broken and there was blood everywhere. The two guys tried to be helpful, but the fire station across the street also provided EMT services so they were on the scene in two minutes or less. With sirens blaring.

Now, I was already embarrassed enough to be at the center of the gathering accident scene. I couldn't see anything without my glasses, so I asked the firemen if they could give me a ride to my house, which was only a mile away. There were two problems with this request, both of which were obvious to the firemen but not to me. One, blood was still coming out of my mouth as I said this. And two, the firemen informed me as soon as they lifted me into the ambulance, they were legally required to take me to an emergency room. Ironically, this was one of the very few mornings where I took off for my run and Elaine said, "Be careful, Dougy," when I actually responded, "Well, you know, I always come home." As the ambulance carted me off to the University of Cincinnati Medical Center Emergency Room, I had to call Elaine and let her know that I would not be returning home unassisted.

As I said, it was a beautiful morning, and it was a Sunday. So, no one was in the emergency room. I seemed to provide a great deal of entertainment to the bored nurses working in ER, as they kept referring to me as "the guy who was out running and fell on his face," which was then followed by giggling. But even with the magnitude of this debacle, my recovery was quick. The next week at work in Ann Arbor even my closest colleagues turned their heads away rather than look at my face. But by the week after that I looked as normal as ever; evidently, facial tissue gets a lot of blood flowing to it and so these kinds of injuries heal quickly. I have made it a point not to fall directly on my face since.

Other than the few times when I've fallen on my face, my only other running injury—knock on wood—was when I used my Christmas break to run hard intervals around the fifth-of-a-mile indoor track at a health club. I got in much better shape that Christmas but it came at a cost. Running hard around the curves created a hernia on my left side. I had to have outpatient surgery one freezing January morning at a Henry Ford outpatient clinic in Michigan to fix the hernia. It was my first ever surgery, so I once again maximized the drama. I acted like I thought I was going to die. In a clear effort to calm me down, my surgeon told me during the pre-op appointment, "Any first-year medical resident could do this surgery, it's that simple." To which I responded, "Well, let's make sure that no first-year resident actually does it." It was a ridiculous injury to have and I felt stupid but I recovered quickly. And I haven't run hard around curves on either an indoor or outdoor track since.

Injuries teach us that we have limits. As a matter of fact, running teaches us that we have limits. Just yesterday I ran nine miles and I wasn't running for time. But after two miles at a slow pace, I ran the last seven miles "fast" (for me). I ended up with a good nine-mile time, at least given my own limits.

We do better when we honor our limits instead of fighting against them. At some point in life, most of us need to deal with the fact that we will never be famous and perhaps also not as rich as we'd like to be—and maybe we are even growing older. Really, we all need to learn that we aren't ever going to get everything we want in life, and to learn to accept that...somehow. Running has taught me what enough means, and how to accept enough with some grace. It's a hard concept to accept in today's world, which seems wired to always getting and having more.

By 1993, I was working in Ann Arbor and living in two places—Cincinnati and Ann Arbor. Elaine was working for the Xavier business school in Cincinnati. Marriages can function in all sorts of ways if you just love each other enough and want to make it work. Most weekends I would drive back and forth—from Ann Arbor to Cincinnati and back to Ann Arbor. Some weekends, Elaine would drive up to Ann Arbor. We ended up living separately during the week for fifteen years, but we only missed being together on the weekends twice—once when I was sick and once due to weather. Somehow this ended up making our marriage stronger, not weaker. Part of it is because we came to value spending time together, perhaps in a way we would not have if we were together all the time. I'm not saying this will work for every marriage, only that it worked for ours.

Most people who work in a different city than their "permanent" home think about it like they have a long commute to work. They end up living out of a hotel or a corporate apartment. That would never have worked for me. I needed to think about it like I lived in two places, and this helped me to create my own life in Ann Arbor. A lot of this was about small things that added up to bigger things. I learned where to find a cheap and fast but good dinner. I joined a health club. I resisted the corporate apartment thing, so that I could feel like Elaine and I had our own place. I met a great friend, Clark, and we worked together at two different companies. And, of course, I figured out where to run.

However, I didn't see much of Ann Arbor other than my office building by I-94 until I signed up for the Big Ten Run, a ten-miler that they used to hold every fall. The race started out on State Street near Yost Ice Arena, where the university hockey team played. Some guy who looked like he had been drinking the night before staggered out onto the porch of one of the old houses that have since been rightfully torn down and played "The Star-Spangled Banner" on his trumpet before the race. We took off up State Street going north, taking a left onto Packard and then a right onto Main Street. I was running at an even, brisk pace, but I had seen Main Street before. Things got more interesting when we crossed over the Huron River to the north side of town and then took a sharp right by the U-M medical school. We ran down Fuller Avenue by the soccer fields and then cut back on a path towards the Huron River.

Now we were on a bike path away from the road, with the river to our right and sparse woods on our left. The pack had thinned out by then but I was still running well, around eight-minute miles. After a mile down the bike path, we crossed over the railroad tracks (that I later learned can take you all the way to Chicago on Amtrak). We ran up Geddes Road, which is either one big, long hill or three steep mini-hills connected by a few plateaus, depending on how you think about it. Either way, it's over a mile of uphill running. I had slowed down but was still holding a decent pace.

We crested the top of the hill at Geddes Road, finally, and turned right through a couple of gates and onto a dirt path. We were running on the top of a ridge; as I glanced to the right I could look down a steep hill and see the Huron River in the distance. We were inside the University of Michigan Arboretum (known locally as "the Arb"), which I didn't even know existed until this moment. It was a gorgeous fall day: cool in a pristine, invigorating way. As the path cut downhill, I lengthened my stride. I was now running a faster pace—about seven-and-a-half-minute miles—and feeling great.

At the bottom of the hill we cut sharply left away from the river; there was a large flower garden to my left. We ran up a short, steep hill and out of the Arb. We were back on central campus. After another short but steep uphill, we cut through campus and ran back to State Street. I was struggling now to hang onto my pace. Once we hit State Street we turned right towards the outdoor U-M track and finished the race with a quarter lap on the track. I'd run ten miles quite a bit faster than I thought I could.

The Big Ten Run was a wonderful way to see Ann Arbor for the first time. I was impressed in a way that you can only be when you see unexpected beauty. It's amazing how much better things can look on a cool fall day rather than during the grey winter, which I later realized Ann Arbor has plenty of. In all the years I was living in Ann Arbor, I ran many interesting races and had regular runs later on much of the same course that the Big Ten Run had covered that day. I ran a beautiful half marathon, several times, from Dexter to Ann Arbor that followed a winding road down the Huron River Valley.

For me, that Big Ten Run was about learning how to love a place for the first time, and nothing can quite match that feeling.

7

THE FLYING PIG MARATHONS

C *incinnati, Ohio, 1999, 2000, 2001*

"It is not the critic who counts. . . . The credit belongs to the man who is actually in the arena, whose face is marred by dust and sweat and blood; who strives valiantly . . . and who at the worst, if he fails, at least fails while daring greatly, so that his place shall never be with those cold and timid souls who know neither victory or defeat."
Theodore Roosevelt

MY JOB IN ANN ARBOR—THE one that had all sorts of red flags when I took it—wasn't working out. After a couple of years, we closed our doors in the summer of 1995. Not on purpose. What started out as a "learning experience" for me, working for a CEO who promised to change but was unable to, ended up being a "Hey, we missed payroll" experience. Which was a different kind of learning experience.

We tried all sorts of ways to raise money for the business, and succeeded for a while, but the day finally came when the CEO had to get up in front of the company and let everyone know we could not meet payroll. It was one of those days you never forget: there isn't a more unambiguous form of business failure than missing payroll. But the empty feeling in my stomach only lasted for a day or two. As much as I had worried about not paying our employees when it became obvious that we couldn't turn the corner into the wonderful land of positive cash flow, everyone except the CEO got new jobs immediately, especially the software developers.

The good news is that I used this unique form of "opportunity" to finally land a job in healthcare information technology. I didn't fully understand it at the time, but I'd been trying to get back into a healthcare tech company for more than five years. And it definitely wasn't a straight-line path that got me the job. I was running at a health club in Ann Arbor in 1993 or '94 when I noticed a classmate of mine from Stanford, Teresa, running on the treadmill next to me. She told me that her husband, Shelby, was starting a new business line inside a healthcare tech company called Medstat. I spent the next two years trying to have lunch with Shelby, despite the fact that we were both working in Ann Arbor. He can be slightly absentminded. One time I was even at the restaurant for lunch when his admin assistant called to let me know he couldn't make it.

By then, I was ready for a new adventure and ready to turn the page. I wasn't down on myself despite the failure of the business, since I knew I had given it everything that I had and felt I could legitimately blame our failure on the CEO, who couldn't get along with anyone. That made me feel better, at least. I was only out of work for about a week and was three weeks from heading back to Cincinnati, since having two places of residence and no paycheck wasn't a sensible money management equation, when Elaine and I ran into Shelby at the coffee shop named Expresso Royale in Ann Arbor. He invited me to lunch—again. After two years of trying to have lunch with him just one time, I ended up having lunch with Shelby every day for a week.

Shelby and his team couldn't quite figure out what to do with me. I didn't have deep "healthcare experience" at that time, nor did I have a stellar track record. What I had was some small-company-building business experience that I thought they needed, and Shelby agreed with that—even though no one else on his team seemed to value that experience. Finally, after enough lunches, I suggested that we start out with a three-month no-strings-attached consulting gig, where I would help him and the team define a business strategy. I argued that this would give both of us a chance to assess if we wanted to work together longer term.

The consulting gig was a great idea. I was able to help them formulate a clear strategy for entering what we then called the "healthcare decision support market" for government agencies. I know that sounds boring, but to me it was a blast. They needed strategic clarity and I was able to help them achieve it. They needed the clarity both to guide their market entry as well as to procure investment money from their parent company, Medstat. We were aiming to create a new market rather than to gain share in an existing one, which is always more fun in a tech business. Plus, the people that I was working with were smart. I ended up signing up for a full-time role after the three-month consulting gig was up.

The first year of that new job felt like not working at all. I had managed to get a director-level strategy job with no direct reports. After many years of having lots of people working for me, the only person I had to manage for a while was myself. Instead, I got to do things like attend conferences and learn about healthcare policy. During one such conference in Portland, I called up Elaine and reported back, "I can't believe that they are paying me for this."

The other thing was that Shelby, despite his absentmindedness, was in his own way a great leader. He had an ego, but could laugh at himself. He didn't mind it when those of us working for him had conflict, even with him, and he encouraged us to debate things before we did them. This led to much better decisions because we were all smart enough to know that our collective knowledge exceeded that of any one of us. It was the first time I ever worked on a management team that was truly functional and able to make decisions and then adjust course as needed. The business started to gain traction and, as it did, my role developed to manage people and do more real work.

I continued to split my time between Ann Arbor and Cincinnati, since Elaine was still working in Cincinnati. I had this plan in my head that we could get our house paid off in Cincinnati and then we would always have a roof over our heads no matter what else happened. Sometimes the foggiest of plans actually work out: by 1997 we were out from under our mortgage. I've never thought seriously about selling our house since. My parents' issues with managing their money made me conservative about managing mine, and Elaine is the master at finding cheap deals. She comes from the western side of Cincinnati, and in keeping with that culture she thinks nothing of spending ten dollars of gas money to save five dollars on a purchase. To her that makes perfect sense.

Most Sundays when I was in Cincinnati, I would take off for a long run from Hyde Park down to Eden Park—and sometimes I even extended the run into Mount Adams. The beautiful wide streets of Hyde Park are an invitation to start running. It's a mile and a half from our house in East Hyde Park to the actual Hyde Park Square. There you can find some decent retail, most notably Graeter's Ice Cream, which is definitively the best ice cream in the world (French press, old-fashioned style). After the square, I head for Madison Avenue and take a left down the rolling hills and through O'Bry-onville, the small village highlighted by Bob Roncker's Running Spot. Then it's through Walnut Hills, which houses some of the largest old mansions in the city. Once I pass by the firehouse on the left and head up to DeSales Corner, things get a bit edgier.

Cincinnati—like many midwestern cities—is still quite racially segregated, and after DeSales Corner the blocks change quickly, back and forth. On the corner of Madison and William Howard Taft Road there is a United Dairy Farmers carryout, which I think of as a Gatorade stop with no restroom. As I head up to Eden Park, I am rewarded with one of the better views of the riverfront from the east side of the city. I run down past the Cincinnati Arboretum, by the large pond and up the hill, and if I still have the energy, into Mount Adams.

Mount Adams, one of the seven hills of Cincinnati, looks almost straight downhill onto downtown. Something like a hundred years ago there was a trolley that connected downtown to Mount Adams. Just past the art museum, I cut up a small but steep hill on the left by Playhouse in the Park, a local live theater house; once you crest that hill just past the Playhouse, you run downhill and head back through Eden Park to home. Thirteen miles in all, with one or two Gatorade stops depending on how hot it is outside.

I am still most comfortable running by myself; since Stanford I have never gotten into training with a group. I am an introvert by nature, like most runners. But sometime during these years I started running occasionally with a small group of hardcore runners. You can meet a lot of interesting characters this way. One such character was a guy named Tom Possert, who back then was the reigning US champion in twenty-four-hour racing. As in, how many miles can you run around a track in twenty-four hours, assuming you are wacky enough to consider doing such a thing? Tom did 142 miles out in California shortly before I met him to win the race. Even worse, he told me that he basically flew out to California, did the twenty-four-hour race, and flew home without seeing any other part of California.

Perhaps inevitably, someone in Cincinnati came up with the idea of hosting a large downtown marathon called the Flying Pig. Historically, when Cincinnati was still vying with Chicago for being the major trading center in the Midwest—a battle that the city obviously lost—it was called "Porkopolis," as it was the country's chief hog-packing center, and herds of pigs roamed the streets. About twenty years ago, when the historical nickname fell back into favor, there were pig statues all over town. The first Flying Pig was run in 1999. Over the years the Flying Pig has gained a reputation as a great beginner's marathon, more about fun-running than competition. It's also gotten much, much larger than that inaugural run.

After many years of "staying in shape," I was once again ready to forget the fact that I had quit marathoning for good. I had forgotten

the agony of the New York and Columbus marathons—so I signed up
for the inaugural Pig.

FLYING PIG MARATHON, May 1999, 4 hours, 34 minutes, 57 seconds

IN ITS INAUGURAL year the Flying Pig starts and finishes at Union
Terminal, a beautiful old railroad station turned into a museum on
the far west side of downtown. This is the first and only year that
Union Terminal will be used as the host site for The Pig. In future
years, as the race grows, it will be run from Sawyer Point, a large
urban park on the Ohio riverfront.

The Pig begins by making a token gesture to Kentucky.
Northern Kentucky is always an afterthought to Cincinnati, which
manages to mostly ignore that its airport, many of its better restau-
rants, and much of its population actually lives in Kentucky. After a
mile or so of wandering around the Ohio side of downtown, we
cross the bridge into Kentucky, then run about two miles there
before crossing back into Ohio. The crowd is especially noisy in
Kentucky, where they also seem to know how to party better than
Ohio does. Especially at 7:00 a.m. on a Sunday. There are a few
bands blasting rock music at these ridiculously early hours. This
shakes me out of my morning stupor, a mixed blessing indeed.
Sometimes it's better to cover five or six miles of the marathon
before you wake up to the full awareness of what you are doing. I
realize rather alarmingly that the problem with bridges over big
rivers like the Ohio is that no matter how flat the bridge seems
when you drive over it, it's pretty hilly when you run over it. Hardly
a brilliant revelation but then again it is only 7:00 a.m. on a
Sunday.

After four or five miles, we are back in Ohio. From downtown we
cut up a huge hill into Eden Park, a pleasant city park that sits at the
foot of Mount Adams. I'm not ready for such a big hill and I start to
worry I am frying my legs like I did in New York. Experience in

marathoning cuts both ways—you may be able to avoid some mistakes but you are also fully aware how fatal they can be.

Once we get up into Eden Park, we reach the rolling hills on Victory Parkway and Madison Avenue, heading through O'Bry-onville. Now I am running a route that I have done many Sundays before in Cincinnati, the only difference being that this time I have a couple of thousand people with me—plus, I can run in the middle of the street. It's awesome. We run by the nursing home in O'Bryonville and they've got folks in wheelchairs cheering for us. We come down off Madison Avenue onto Erie, headed for Hyde Park Square. The crowds start thickening and, while it's certainly not First Avenue in New York, they are making quite a bit of noise. Plus, I'm on my home turf. The adrenaline rush is real enough.

Once we hit the corner of Paxton Avenue and Erie, we take a left on Paxton, run by Kroger and then down Wasson Avenue—a light industrial street with some ugly condos on the corner of Wasson and Marburg. There aren't too many people on Wasson and there's not much to look at, but there are plenty of port-o-lets here. I realize it's a good place to have them as I cruise by, noting that the race is well organized for a first marathon.

We turn right on Marburg and then left back on Erie Avenue: now we are in my neighborhood. Elaine has walked the block from our house to hang out and watch the race and give me a PowerBar as I run by. I'm glad to see her but there is no big reason to make a public display of that; I give her a quick hug and tell her I love her and grab the PowerBar. I know she is worried that I will keel over before I finish but I don't say anything. This isn't a good time for big conversations.

I'm flying as I head down Erie past Hyde Park Country Club towards Red Bank Road. Now I'm almost at the fourteen-mile mark and running in decent pace and cadence. I'm in that delusional place where in your head you think you can run forever. Reality strikes when we don't head directly to the nice part of Mariemont but instead head down Bramble Avenue, which has both hills and potholes. As in potholes to twist your ankle in if you are not careful.

Why did they route the course this way? I shove that thought out of my mind as we wind through Mariemont, heading for Lunken Airport. Once we get there, we are on Eastern Avenue.

Eastern Avenue is the place that makes or breaks your Pig run most years. It's one of those cool rehab districts where you think it would be great to hang out, but you never go—unless you happen to be running The Pig. It's also long, lasting four or five miles, and it can seem interminable if you start crashing here. This year we are covering miles fifteen to twenty; I can't quite make up my mind if it's hilly. Every time I feel halfway decent there is another hill to climb; but there are also a few gradual downhills where I can relax and maintain my pace. I render the verdict that I am on rolling hills, which calms me down. I am also starting to feel it; it's a hot day and I've never fully trained for these damn marathons. I start slowing my pace; not to a marathon shuffle, but I might be heading there. All marathons eventually reduce you down to the next moment and next step, and nothing more or less than that.

After Eastern Avenue we cut through downtown and jog through some heavy industrial areas on the near west side of downtown. The crowds are scarce to nonexistent and my legs are telling me they are cooked. Finally, I see Union Terminal and the finish line. I'm on my feet but running very slow. I cross in four hours and thirty-four minutes: not great but semi-respectable. And I've avoided a total collapse on my limited training.

FLYING PIG MARATHON, *May 2000, 4 hours, 22 minutes, 56 seconds*

I'M NOT ENAMORED with my inaugural Pig run, but for whatever reason, I seem to be into running marathons again. I decide to train harder for the second year of The Pig. For better or worse, I also enlist the help of my stepson, Rik, who is getting his undergrad degree at the University of Cincinnati. I call Rik up the night before the race and ask him if he can bring me a Gatorade bottle at the mile seventeen mark, since that seems strategically important and I have studied the race course enough to know I will be downtown then— and only a few miles from where Rik lives.

I don't think that I am making a special request of Rik or anything, but based on his reaction—which is a fascinating combination of silence and unenthusiastic trepidation—I can tell that I am asking him to do something that is difficult for him. As if I just asked him to run the whole marathon with me. Then I realize that I will be passing the seventeen-mile mark around 9:30 a.m., which is crazy early for Rik on a Sunday morning. (Never mind the fact that I will have already been up for four hours, three of which I have spent running my brains out.) I am reminded of the time when Rik got back to our Ann Arbor apartment at 5:00 a.m., and decided to play offense rather than defense. Before we could hammer him for all of our worry about where the heck he'd been, he explained to us with Einstein-like rigor, "Well, there are lunar people and solar people. And you guys are solar and I am lunar." This message was delivered with the certainty of a mathematical proof.

The actual race day for the second Pig is cooler than the first Pig. They have moved the race up to the first Sunday in May, and the week-earlier race day makes a significant difference. (The Pig has stuck with the first Sunday in May ever since.) I am determined to run at an even pace and I take off as if I can do so. The voice inside me is reminding me to breathe nice and easy.

Suddenly, on crossing back into Ohio on one of the bridges at about the three-mile mark, my stomach is feeling queasy. A half mile later, on Second Street in downtown, I am thinking I might throw up right in the middle of the street. A few hundred yards after that I am positive I am going to throw up. I can't tell if it's just nerves or something that I ate. I decide to bet on nerves and I manage to calm myself down. The feeling passes by the time I hit the five-mile mark.

Now I am back on the familiar part of the course. The Pig has changed the first few miles and the last few over the years but the middle of the course is always the same—up from downtown to Eden Park, up Victory Parkway to Madison Avenue, through O'Bryonville to Hyde Park Square, down Erie to Mariemont, by Lunken Airport to Eastern Avenue, deal with the rolling hills on Eastern Avenue until you hit downtown again. This year the weather is better and the crowds are noisier and thicker. More people are catching onto the race as a community event.

Around the sixteen-mile mark, I start wondering if Rik woke up on time to buy a Gatorade bottle and make his way downtown. Which I now realize is a considerable task for him. It would be great to see him but also, I need the Gatorade. By the seventeen-mile mark I am fading and he is nowhere to be found. *Oh well,* I think, *he must have just slept in; it's not that big of deal, he's just a college kid with a big fro, especially for a white guy. You can only expect so much.* Then suddenly at 17.2 miles there he is, screaming, "Go, Doug!" And with the Gatorade. I pick up my stride and grab the Gatorade with a quick "Thanks, dude." Now I am pumped up. He's given me a massive turbo boost.

My newfound adrenaline, boosted merely by the presence of Rik, carries me all the way to the finish line, which is now downtown on the riverfront. I cross in it in four hours, twenty-two minutes, and fifty-six seconds. Good enough to finish 2,137th out of 3,633 overall and 268th out of 366 in my age group, just in case anyone other than me cares. And good enough to persuade me to buy the marathon-finisher photo where you can see me crossing the finish line afterwards, even though such things are always a bit of a rip-off.

Being a stepdad can be a strange thing. In many ways you are defined by what you are not. You are not the "real" dad; you are not dealing with the consequences and ramifications of your own genetics; you are not in a position to expect that much. Occasionally, much is expected of you. When the "real" dad turns out to not be, well, not always a very good dad, you need to figure out how to step in. Without being competitive or threatening, but by offering whatever you have to give. Sometimes discipline, sometimes advice, but always friendship and support. You don't always get rewarded for this, at least not in the present moment, but today I have been.

·   ·   ·

FLYING PIG MARATHON, May 2001, 4 hours, 37 minutes, 44 seconds

MY MEMORIES of my third Flying Pig are the sketchiest of all. This might have to do with the hard reality that I crash again. This time, there is no Rik bearing Gatorade. And the organizers have tweaked the course again, this time for the worse. At the sixteen-mile mark, the race has already covered the Eastern Avenue stint, and the rolling hills have taken their toll. But not nearly as much as what is to come.

Cruelly, the course takes off from downtown up Central Parkway towards the University of Cincinnati. Central Parkway has seen better days, especially the part closest to downtown. As we start the uphill climb, I can't imagine going all the way to UC. I hadn't bothered to study the course map too deeply before the race. But the route takes us the whole three and a half miles all the way to the university, uphill the entire way. It feels like a nasty joke.

By the time I get to Clifton, my legs are totally dead. You have to be in great shape to manage a three-and-a-half-mile uphill starting at mile sixteen of any marathon; I am not in great shape. By the time we arrive at the top of Central Parkway at 19.5 miles, I am out of gas—with almost seven miles to go. But that's not the end of it. The course turns west into the rundown industrial part of Cincinnati on the west side of I-75. We wind through streets that I would never go to for any reason during the day or night. There are only scattered spectators, and a few dogs, and they all look nearly as unhappy as I feel.

After enough of this, I give up any pretense of running or looking good. It becomes all about finding a way to the finish line down by the river. Which I finally do in four hours and forty-two minutes, my worst marathon time ever (or at least so far). I am bummed out about the course, bummed out about my time, and burned out on The Pig. I decide to "quit" marathons for good—again.

≈

WHAT WAS GOING on at work undoubtedly didn't help my mental

state at that point. I had left my job at Medstat in the fall of 2000, as I was getting tired of the commute to Ann Arbor and things weren't going all that great. We were in the middle of the dot.com boom, which happened shortly before the dot.com bust. I decided to return to Cincinnati to work for a venture-funded software start-up, running client delivery for them.

I was excited to be back home with Elaine, but that excitement didn't last long. The software company was selling markdown pricing solutions to retailers, which was a big joke on me since I hated shopping and knew nothing about retailers. The job turned out to be a disaster. The Saturday before my first day of work my new boss, the CEO, called me and said, "Hey, we need to go to Green Bay on Monday." So, I met him at the airport and we flew into Chicago and then proceeded to do the five-hour drive north to Green Bay, where our only customer was located. We were on the verge of losing this customer when I discovered that my "team" consisted of contractors who were getting paid quite a lot of money through some other deal —and it felt like winter in Green Bay already.

That was my first day on the job, and things went downhill from there. Our "product" had a back-end algorithm to help calculate the markdowns, but no real presentable "front end" that a customer could actually use. So, my services team ran the product every week for our customers, some of whom weren't paying customers. The magnitude of that problem was reinforced to me one day when I went to visit one of our customers, Meijer, in Grand Rapids, Michigan. After making small talk about golf with our key contact for about twenty minutes, since I couldn't figure out what else to talk about, the guy finally asked, "So, what can I do for you?"

"Well, I'd like to know what you think of our product," I mumbled.

"What product?" was his memorable response.

That was a clue that things weren't going too well. To make up for the mess of the software product, the culture of the company was also a mess, mostly because it was run by a bunch of guys in Cincinnati who mistakenly weren't really open to advice from anyone else. Eventually, the investors brought in the consulting firm McKinsey to come up with a strategy for the company, but the even one of the best management consulting firms in the world couldn't change anyone's mind in Cincinnati.

One Friday night I was stuck at work because we couldn't even get our back-end software—the part of the product that we actually had —to work, and Elaine called me. The CEO of Medstat had called my home asking if I was interested in coming back to Ann Arbor. The timing was perfect. It was one of the better breaks of my career, and within two months I was back in Ann Arbor.

8

THE FLYING PIG REVISITED

C incinnati, Ohio, May 2006, 4 hours, 41 minutes, 32 seconds

You are a child of the universe,
no less than the trees and the stars;
you have a right to be here.
And whether or not it is clear to you,
no doubt the universe is unfolding as it should.

Therefore be at peace with God,
whatever you conceive Him to be.
And whatever your labors and aspirations,
in the noisy confusion of life,
keep peace with your soul.

With all its sham, drudgery, and broken dreams,
it is still a beautiful world.
Be cheerful. Strive to be happy.

Max Ehrmann, Desiderata

ON SEPTEMBER 10, 2001, I rejoined Medstat in Ann Arbor. I was excited to be back working with great people and selling into an industry that I actually cared about. It was always easier for me to get interested in healthcare, where you were dealing with something that involved real people, rather than something like financial services, where I wasn't so sure.

The next day during a relatively mundane management team meeting, an admin assistant broke into the meeting room, much to the dismay of my boss who valued order above all else, to tell us about planes crashing into the World Trade Center in New York City. This sounded odd. Work resumed as before, but by the time I went out to lunch it was clear the United States had been attacked by terrorists. It was a sunny early fall day in Ann Arbor. I had a hard time wrapping my brain around the fact that something bad was happening in New York. It seemed unreal.

That night, I went back to my ugly hotel room at the Extended Stay America that was squeezed between the Briarwood Mall and I-94. I felt a desperate need to talk to Elaine and to Rik, who was then living in Chicago. As Rik expressed his worries about our country and the state of the world, I found, much to my despair, that I could not offer reassurance. It would not be the last time that I couldn't reassure him about the future state of the world.

By now I understood that nothing in life was going to be perfect. When I went back to Medstat, Elaine was still working in Cincinnati and I was still doing some consulting there, while working half-time at Medstat. I rented a cozy cottage on a small, muddy lake ten miles north of Ann Arbor, close to Whitmore Lake, a much nicer location.

The cottage was either charming or dilapidated, depending on your point of view. My own inclination that it was charming started to fray around the edges when, more than once, I got up around midnight in the middle of winter and the heater wasn't working. It was too cold to sleep, so I went back to Ann Arbor and checked into the Holiday Inn around 2:00 a.m. Despite this, my job was going well. I decided to use my internal political chips at the company to carve out a focus on innovation at Medstat, which worked out because nearly everyone else at the place was too risk-averse. It's always more fun to create something new than try to improve upon an existing product or process.

After nine months, we bought a small condo in Ann Arbor and I closed the door on that "cozy" cottage. My new home was a low-end condo where medical residents might live, but it did have a few redeeming qualities. Or, I should say, redeeming to me. Mainly, it was right up the hill from Argo Livery and the Huron River. Once I walked down to the river, I could run as far as I wanted, especially if I headed east to Gallup Park. Ann Arbor is just as good a running city as Cincinnati but in a different way—less urban, with easier access to the river, and much flatter, with hills being more an optional feature than a requirement on long runs. The thrill of running big, steep hills had long since evaporated.

As I neared my fiftieth birthday, I started to focus more on what I wanted to check off my bucket list. I still hadn't gotten to all fifty states and won my contest with Chris, my friend from Stanford. So, in 2005 we went to Hawaii and stayed on Maui and then the Big Island, where my brother Scott lives in Kona. Hawaii is one of those places that lives up to the hype: a stunningly magical combination of ocean, rugged beaches, rainforests, and mountains. Hawaii knocked off my forty-ninth state and then in 2006, right after I turned fifty, we went to Alaska to make it fifty states.

I was going to run the Anchorage Marathon in June 2006, but that May we were in Cincinnati for Flying Pig weekend and the weather forecast was for agreeably cool running weather in the fifties and low sixties. I started thinking about how great it would be to just enjoy Alaska rather than having to run 26.2 miles there. So, the Saturday before The Pig I told Elaine that I "might" run the actual marathon the next day rather than the half, and I went down and signed up for the full marathon race too. Of course, I totally knew by then I was going to do the whole enchilada—I just wasn't quite ready to tell Elaine that. Why waste all my training and the great weather?

～

BY THE TIME I get to The Pig starting line, I have let go of all goals of running fast. Or any notion that someday I might be fast enough to qualify for Boston (three hours and thirty minutes for my current age group). I decide I am running this marathon "for fun," or at least my version of fun. I am relaxed, but still respectful of the beast that is a marathon.

My game plan, to the extent that I have one, is simply to put one foot in front of the other for as long as I can. I don't want to walk. Over ten years have passed since my debacle in New York, but the pain and embarrassment of those last eight miles in the Bronx and Central Park are still stuck in my brain. Right there along with the rocks in my brain that caused me to run marathons in the first place, especially doing one to celebrate my fiftieth birthday.

We begin with the ritualistic, token-gesture run over to Kentucky and back. Once that's out of the way and we climb the hill up into Eden Park, I'm feeling okay. We continue up to Victory Parkway and then hit the rolling hills on Madison. Through O'Bryonville I maintain a relaxed, even pace. I hit Erie and Hyde Park Square as if I was out on a slow Sunday morning stroll, yet taking in the crowds and feeding off their energy.

Right around the thirteen-mile mark we turn the corner at Erie and Marburg and there, after we pass Dutch's carryout store is Elaine, as always. Holding a PowerBar, another Gatorade, and urging me to "be careful, Dougy." Whatever else I've done, I've managed to marry a fantastic woman. A lot of it was just sheer dumb luck.

Down Erie to Murray Avenue I'm flying, past the fourteen-mile mark. We wind around Mariemont for a while, seeming to add distance so that we don't have to do so much crazy stuff at the end around the river. The voice in my head is now active and engaged; I know this is crunch time. *Just stay on your feet, Doug, just keep going. Run as far as you can.* I'm holding a steady pace, doing a slow fade of no more than ten seconds each mile. We hit the sixteen-mile mark on Route 50 pulling out of Mariemont. I haven't broken my pace, other than a few water stops, the whole race.

We go down onto Eastern Avenue and head right to Bella Luna, the Italian place I ate at the night before the race. I am right where I want to be, right where I belong. We are closing in on eighteen miles, and I am still running strong. Eastern Avenue and the rolling hills; I am no longer intimidated by these miles. Just past the twenty-mile mark, I know I've got it. There will be no crashing today for this fifty-year-old, nothing to be ashamed of. Even though my fifty-year-old body starts talking to me, mostly by stiffening up, my mind is rock-solid. Nothing but positive self-talk.

Before I know it, I am within a mile of the finish line. The endorphins are flowing into my brain big-time, to the point of reality distortion. I know that I have slowed down, a lot, but my brain is still messaging to me that I am feeling good. I start to wonder how I might look. I tell myself I must be looking good. As soon as I have that thought, a medic rides up on a bike and asks me if I can make it to the finish line. Maybe I'm not looking so good after all.

I tell the medic I am totally fine; he and I both know I am lying. I cross the finish line. I have been running the entire race except water stops, at least by some forgiving definition of running. I finish in four hours and forty-one minutes, which places me in the back half of the pack of marathon finishers. Of course, that doesn't count all the fifty-year-old guys who would never attempt a marathon.

~

FIFTY IS NOT THE "NEW FORTY" or anything like that. That's marketing stuff invented to sell stuff to baby boomers. In your fifties you know that you are firmly in the middle of your life, if not closer to the end. One of the things about middle age is you start to think more about life's constraints and limitations—not in the abstract sense, but your own life's constraints. Some things become obvious. I won't become CEO of a large corporation. I will never qualify for the Boston Marathon. Some things are easier to accept than others. I never wanted to run a large company in the first place; who would want to make all those trade-offs? I valued having time to myself too much to have my schedule always defined by some large company.

Some things are harder to accept. I grew up as a child of the sixties, and I've never lost the idea that I wanted to change the world for the better. And I haven't done that in a fundamental way. The world is, if anything, more broken than ever. Certainly, the country is more polarized culturally and politically—and the American dream remains elusive to way too many people. Where you are born and who your parents are and who you know and what color your skin is —these things still matter way more than they should.

I'm getting better at realizing when enough is enough. I am no longer the "young smart guy with potential." I'm the guy in the middle of every-thing with demands coming from all sides. Gratitude has turned out to be more important than I ever thought it was. Small things—like what we do with today—have turned out to be a bigger deal than I ever thought. Maybe the small things are in fact the things that matter most in life.

Frustrated with my work-life balance, I sign up for life-coaching sessions from a guy in his twenties who is surprisingly mature. During one of our phone sessions, I blurt out, "I just want to make every day count." I pause and wonder if I may have actually said something profound.

In March 2007, I am at a conference in New Orleans on health-care technology. Elaine is with me; it's a combo of professional trip and mini-vacation. I get a message from my boss that suggests she is about ready to get fired or leave. Stuff like this happens all the time at a big company like Thomson Reuters, but never to me or my boss. And I like working for her.

I return to Ann Arbor a few days later and she tells me she's been fired. It has nothing to do with "performance" and everything to do with politics, which in a way is part of performance in a large company. It's time for me to step up, to get the bigger job, to figure out how to make it all work. I'm nervous, but I will learn over the next four years that I am finally ready. I deal with tons of corporate stuff; the stuff that I always previously worked hard to avoid having to deal with.

In early February 2008 I get a very different phone call. My sister Robin has ovarian cancer; she finds out the day before her fifty-fifth birthday. Everyone is devastated—my mom, my dad, her twin sister Susan, and of course, Robin. We drive to Columbus and I cry a few times. The twins live and work together and we all always thought of them as having identical life experiences, which they seemed to want, but God—or whomever—has other plans. It is stage III ovarian cancer and I know what that means. I work with a bunch of doctors and nurses. It has already spread and the prognosis for longer-term survival is not good.

We all fight the good fight in our own way, Robin with the most courage of all. That summer she has surgery at Ohio State, and initially the surgeon is positive. Her blood tests—called CA-125— improve. Then she and Susan go back to "life as normal," but it's anything but normal. They still need to make a living and go back to trying to run their travel agency. They start eating better stuff, but their core life stresses—money, my parents, time demands—have not changed. I try to help, but often feel hopeless, especially when I try to get my sisters, who have always been highly strung, to manage "stress" better.

My parents and sisters have always thought my running thing was weird and have been convinced that I would probably just fall over— sooner rather than later. Perhaps this is just a defense mechanism on their part, since they are all kind of overweight. They think being thin is the worst thing in the world healthwise—I think they are wrong but I give up on trying to tell them about that.

I do what I can for Robin, which is mostly spend money to try to help. My friend Alan's wife works as a doctor at MD Anderson in Houston. I get my sisters an appointment with one of the best ovarian cancer doctors in America. She is hopeful but ultimately cannot change the course of the disease.

By Christmastime 2008 it is clear that Robin is sick, again. She and Susan show up for Christmas with sunglasses on, but it's easy to see past the disguise that Robin is the sick one. I still have the picture at home to prove it. There is the superficial and then there is the real—the reality is that Robin is dying and I realize that.

By the summer of 2009 fluid is starting to fill up her lungs, which is not at all a good sign. I learn that there is always a surgeon willing to offer hope and to operate, not necessarily in that order. Robin starts to come to grips with her impending death, with courage beyond what I can grasp. Susan refuses to accept the course of the disease, and understandably so—to nearly everyone but me, most especially themselves, the twins have always been one unit and not two. It's impossible for my sisters to conceptualize life without each other.

By late July the trajectory is clear. Still, one day I get a hopeful voicemail from Robin about her next surgery to drain the fluid from her lungs—which I hang onto for the next five years and replay when I want to hear her voice again—until I have to switch phone services.

A week before she dies, Elaine and I go to visit Robin at Riverside Hospital in Columbus. We all know where this is headed and we manage to talk about it as a family, in our own way. I make jokes about how Susan can move to Hawaii to live with my brother Scott after Robin is gone, and Robin laughs genuinely and graciously. Of course, like most of the jokes in my family, they weren't totally jokes. We go back to Ann Arbor and I try to focus on work. By Friday I know that the end is near, so I call Susan and Robin, who by now are in a hospice. Although I usually do my weekend work in Ann Arbor at Zingerman's Deli on Sunday morning, this week I get my work done on Saturday afternoon.

On early Sunday morning, September 20, 2009, Robin dies. She is fifty-six years old. Mom calls me at 6:30 a.m. I go to Zingerman's at 7:00 a.m. to collect my usual coffee and muffin before we head for Columbus. The only other customer in the store is a young father with twin daughters in a stroller. They are dressed the same: something I never thought was a good idea for Susan and Robin, not that anyone cared what I thought. I have no idea how to construct the words; the father looks at me and simply says, "We don't normally dress them alike." I still don't know what to say, so I nod and say nothing. I'm not going to mess with this guy's day by telling him my sister just died.

Elaine and I head for Columbus. It's a beautiful fall morning, other than that thing about my sister just dying. We stop at a rest area south of Findlay so that I can call Chris and make the football picks. We make our picks every Sunday morning during NFL season no matter what else is going on—the day after his son was born, the day my sister dies, whatever.

We go to my mom and dad's condo, which we bought for them when they moved to Columbus to work at my sisters' travel agency. Susan has been telling us for months that she doesn't want to live without Robin. We try to talk to my mom about it. Finally, after a couple of hours, Elaine and I drive the twenty minutes to Susan and Robin's condo. Elaine won't let me go inside; instead, she goes in. I expect to lose my second sister on the same day. Instead, Susan has taken a bunch of pills but is still breathing. We call 911 and they show up right away. The emergency techs tell us Susan will be okay and haul her off in an ambulance. The cops show up and head into the condo. They keep coming out, telling me that there are two of everything arranged symmetrically in the condo. I already know all that stuff and I don't feel like talking about it right now.

We head back to Riverside Hospital to make sure that Susan is admitted. They ask me at the hospital if I want to go see Susan right now. The answer is no. The next morning it starts raining in

Columbus and the monsoon lasts through Robin's funeral the following Saturday. Finally, on Saturday evening we start heading back to Ann Arbor and, just south of Bowling Green, the rain finally stops. There is a clear and full rainbow in the sky as we drive north on I-75. I am not religious but it's hard to process this as anything other than a sign from Robin. There's a football game going on at Bowling Green State University, where we all grew up. They are playing Boise State. We stop and watch the game, but by the end of the first half BG is down by more than forty points.

Elaine and I get back on the highway to head back to Ann Arbor. Life is not the same and it won't ever be the same. But it will go on.

And I will go on.

9

HALF MARATHON MAN

"You've got to invest in the world, you've got to read, you've got to go to art galleries, you've got to find out the names of plants. You've got to start to love the world and know about the whole genius of the human race. We're amazing people."
Vivienne Westwood

MY MARATHON-RUNNING career might be over, but my half-marathon career is not. The half seems like the perfect distance. Let's face it, the second half of the marathon doesn't do anything good for your health. It's just more pounding. Plus, and it's taken me way too long to figure this out, when you run the half you can actually take a shower and still have time to watch the marathoners finish while you are eating lunch with your spouse.

There's a club for people who have finished marathons in all fifty states. I've decided I will never be part of that club. It's a good thing; they are almost certainly a bunch of nut jobs. Instead, I'm trying to run a half or a full in half of the states. Some people are happy as long as they have a to-do list in front of them; it doesn't matter that much what's on it.

I think I ran my first half in Golden Gate Park when I was at Stanford. I am not sure how long it took me but it wasn't long compared to what it would take me now. Running is a great way to see new cities and I've seen plenty of them on foot—New York, London, Chicago, Denver, New Orleans, Seattle, Boston, Washington DC, even Victoria, BC. You have no excuse for missing the scenery when you are on foot. But no city is better to see on foot than San Francisco, especially when you find your way to Golden Gate Park.

Back in 2000 I had a good friend who lived in Boise. He invited us to run some half marathons and to come see him. We took a four-day weekend and flew into Spokane and met him forty-five minutes from the airport in Coeur d'Alene, Idaho, a fascinating combination of Idaho-rich and Idaho-redneck-poor. The place had a cool main drag with lots of down-and-out stuff around it. There was a flat-out-and-back course right next to the pristine mountain lake. And after you've done a bunch of marathons the half doesn't seem like it's too long.

The next year, we flew into Boise and I did a half there too, so that I have both sides of Idaho pretty much covered. Especially when you realize that about 90 percent of the state is mountains. The day before that race I took Elaine on a scenic ride up to McCall at seven thousand plus feet and then to some place called Warm Lake. Warm Lake wasn't one of my better ideas: after several twists and turns up the mountain we were on impassable roads covered with snow and ice in a rental car, and I had to figure out how to do a U-turn. There were quite a few pickup trucks up there, most certainly holding people with guns. And it wasn't warm either; Elaine was unhappy with me.

In the fall of 2006, I got it into my head that I should attempt to reprise my performance in the Avenue of the Giants Marathon from when I was at Stanford. Never mind the fact that I was twenty years older, that I was working more than full-time, and that I had crashed when I ran the Avenue of the Giants the first time. All of that was tossed aside, thanks to a foggy memory and a strong sense of nostalgia. At least I had the sense to sign up for the half rather than the full marathon. Elaine and I flew into San Francisco, shortly after this idea flew into my head, for a four-day weekend. We went to see my friend Mike and his wife in Los Altos. Then we headed north for the redwoods.

It was a longer drive up than my nostalgia had allowed and there was a lot more traffic than I remembered. But when I got to our "hotel"—more or less a cabin about twenty-five miles from the actual start of the race—it was like nothing had changed in twenty years. At the start of the half marathon, which also served as the start of the real marathon, I glanced around me at my fellow racers and—as I mentioned before—they were all incredibly fit. It is a race that no one runs by accident, since it is many miles from wherever you happen to live. But the redwoods retain their majesty and are the star of the show. There were some miles early in the race where I felt like I was still in my thirties. And then after struggling in the last few miles—it's almost impossible not to go out too fast in chilly weather on a course this majestic—I managed to finish in a decent time. The reward after the run of the long trip back to the Bay Area through the Russian River Valley was only slightly diminished by running the half rather than the full marathon.

In the midst of Robin's cancer treatments in March of 2009, I had a minor health crisis of my own. I managed to choke on some food in a restaurant in Ann Arbor and, luckily, the guy next to me was a doctor. I hate public displays where I am the center of attention, but when you are choking in the middle of a busy restaurant you become the center of attention whether you want to or not. After the doctor did the Heimlich maneuver on me it seemed like I was okay. But it became clear five weeks later, when I thought that I had a chest cold like everyone else in Ann Arbor in March, that I wasn't okay after all.

The food dislodged from the choking had aspirated into my lung and I had developed a severe lung infection that the emergency room folks at the University of Michigan Hospital originally thought was "just" pneumonia. My good friend Mark tried to tell me after I was discharged from the emergency room that I might have food stuck in my lung but, stupidly, I ignored him and just thought he was being too negative. After all, I had good drugs and there was college basketball on TV in March. Two days later and after struggling to make it up the steps in my condo, I was admitted to the hospital. I ended up having laparoscopic ("non-invasive") surgery in my lungs to clear out the stuff and spending eleven days in the hospital.

Even though I am a total wimp when it comes to health problems, the kind of idiot who thinks he is going to die every time he gets a cold, for some reason I was stoic when faced with a real health situation. The key to that was acceptance; there was a moment before I had surgery when I forgave myself for being so stupid as to think that I just had a chest cold, for doing something as dumb as choking in the middle of a restaurant, and I simply accepted where I was at. Which made all the difference in dealing with my then-dire health situation. Go figure. No one was more surprised than me.

It took me six weeks from my hospital discharge to return to work and, after I recovered my basic functions like breathing normally, it was a glorious time. A couple of my great friends came over to my condo and installed a treadmill. As spring arrived in Ann Arbor, I would walk around the city five or six miles at a time, in no particular hurry to get anywhere. I promised Elaine I would only walk, but one day I was walking down Barton Springs Drive close to the river and I ran about twenty yards. It worked. It was amazing. My version of life includes running, so even twenty yards meant life was coming back.

I spent six months or so making sure I was okay, and getting used to the fact that one clear impact of the chest tubes they slammed into me in the hospital was that my ribs wouldn't be returning to the same place that they were before this whole thing started. Oh well, body symmetry is overrated.

Finally, by early 2010, I was ready to run a race again. I scouted out the spring half marathons in Ohio and decided to sign up for one that I had done a long time ago in Athens, where Ohio University is located. Athens is in the foothills of Appalachia so I knew the course could be hilly, but I figured I needed an excuse anyway if my time wasn't any good. If ever there was a race I ran where just getting to the finish line was the whole point, it was Athens, Ohio, in 2010. I finished in two hours and eleven minutes—almost a ten-minute-per-mile pace—but I was elated to have finished at all. And my lungs were totally intact when I finished. Nothing is better than a good comeback story, especially when you are the one making the comeback.

The next year—in the fall of 2011—I was on my way to grab dinner in Ann Arbor when I got a phone call from Alan, a close friend of mine whom I had worked with for a few years, asking me if I wanted to run a software company in Milwaukee. I was fifty-five and the years at Thomson Reuters were starting to all look alike. When this happens, you know you should probably change something, like your job.

I had always been a great critic of all the CEOs that I had worked for up to this point; it was time to figure out if I could actually run something myself. Analysis can only get you so far when it comes to major life decisions. I read a book once that advised, when facing such choices, to choose the path that will make for the better story. I thought about it for a few weeks, talked to a few of my closest friends in confidence, plus Elaine, and then I went with my gut and took the job. Which doesn't sound like that big of deal but I did answer one big question for myself right out of the chute. I had always wondered if I had the guts to take the risk of signing up to run a company. I did. We were going to Milwaukee and damn the torpedoes.

Elaine and I moved ourselves to Milwaukee, despite not knowing anyone there except the founder whom I was replacing as CEO. He didn't like me much at all back then. The company that I was hired to run was broken, but they already had almost $20 million a year in revenue. I knew that at age fifty-five I would never want to start something from ground zero, but maybe I could take something that already had traction and figure out how to grow the business.

I was partially right about being able to figure it all out. I was CEO of the company for nearly four years, and during that time we brought in new investors, helped old investors (and the founder, who now liked me better) cash out, made a big acquisition, and took the company public through an initial public offering. We were able to grow the business, but we could never quite figure out how to make it profitable. And there's a lot to be said for having positive cash flow, which we didn't have. So, when the dust settled, it wasn't a successful public company. But I built up the team and had an intense CEO experience in every sense of the word, with many tough moments and a few legitimate high points. We even created many good high-tech jobs, at least for a while.

Not surprisingly, my running didn't go any better during this time period, but it kept me hanging in there. It was no longer about goals. Running was now like a lifelong friend that wasn't going to let me down. The first year I was CEO I ran a half marathon in Madison, Wisconsin—it was during a time when we were doing a bunch of public relations stuff for the company and we were in the middle of shooting a video about our company culture. When I disclosed to the company shooting the video that I was running a half marathon that Saturday, they wanted to come and take footage of me at the starting line. They were trying to demonstrate that I was a real human being. Of course, I refused. I didn't want the attention. I wanted to focus on the half marathon and, more importantly, I wanted to keep my running life to myself—like the old friend it was.

I slept badly the night before the race and showed up at the starting line bleary-eyed. To my great chagrin, there at the starting line was the young video guy who had driven the eighty miles from Milwaukee to Madison, according to him without any sleep. I was horrified, but I was polite to him. I knew that someone else had put him up to making the trip. I still hated public scenes, and here I was at the start of the half with all the other runners and some guy taking a video of me. The other runners must have thought I was a total egomaniac. Regardless, it was a fantastic half marathon, downtown Madison being a scenic place, although I faded when I got to the lakeshore near the finish line. I kept running down that lakeshore looking for that finish line, until finally it showed up.

We had several chances to sell the company that I was running and oh, by the way, make quite a bit of money in the process, but the investors didn't want to sell because "things were going so well." This particular problem was not one I'd anticipated before I took the job. I'd played through lots of scenarios in my mind, but never the one where we were "so successful" that we weren't going to be smart enough to cash out when the time was right.

Two and a half years in, we had two potential buyers but, in the end, neither of them actually came through with offers. By mid-2014 we were out of money and, since our investors didn't want to put more money in, our only option for raising more cash (and keeping everyone employed) was to take the company public.

I went for several runs and walks down by Lake Michigan in downtown Milwaukee, during which I came up with a strategy that I thought would be good enough to get the company (and me) to survive the road show and get public. It was, barely. I was only able to survive this process because I had learned, finally, how to calm my mind and slow myself down. I could concentrate when I needed to, yet not worry too much the rest of the time. During the IPO road show in December 2014, I would get up at 4:00 a.m. to run on the hotel treadmill before the long days of pitching the company; that was the only hour of the day when I knew the investment bankers wouldn't be bothering me.

It took considerable adrenaline to get through all this, and once I did get through it I didn't have much energy left. Eight months later we started missing our numbers. The board was clearly getting frustrated with me, and I hadn't quite gotten over how we hadn't sold the company back when we had the chance. So, I decided to fire myself before the board fired me. I kept thinking about how tired I was and how hard I had worked for the last thirty years. I hatched the idea of taking a two-week vacation with Elaine in Mexico, a country I had never been to before. This idea started as a simple mental diversion before becoming an obsession and then an actual plan. It was time to hop off the software-company treadmill. As a matter of fact, it was time to hop off the full-time-work treadmill, period. End of sentence. I managed to recruit my replacement, and to get myself demoted so that I still had a paycheck. Nine months later, I resigned. I didn't have a life plan, beyond the two-week vacation in Mexico. Which seemed like a good enough plan at the time.

Our trip to Mexico was great, except for maybe the part about me trying to drive the rental car. Their version of a "speed bump" was more like an obstruction to tear out the bottom of your car, unless you slowed down to two miles per hour. Which I learned, of course, only after going over a few of those speed bumps too fast; too fast, in this case, being about fifteen miles per hour.

We went to San Miguel de Allende, a beautiful mountain town a few hours north of Mexico City. There was nowhere to run there, especially on the cobblestone streets, unless you went further up the mountain to the public gardens. And even there the trails were short. But we stayed in a cheap and nice hacienda in town and, since we were walking so much, when we got back two weeks later I learned I had lost at least eight pounds. Which was great for dealing with my weight obsession. Plus, eventually, my running.

Other than marathons, I hadn't ever tracked my running times, unlike most obsessive runners. Maybe when I first started out—I can't quite remember—but not in at least thirty years. Somewhat irrationally—well, okay, totally irrationally—I decided a few months before I quit my job to start recording my times for my longer runs. I had somehow acquired the delusional notion that I could get faster in my sixties, since I wouldn't be working full-time. I've always been good at coming up with "plans" that defy reality but this one might take the cake, defying the basics of human biology.

Amazingly, for at least a few months after I stopped working, the plan no-shit-worked. I entered one of those wonderful life time zones where there is no plan other than waking up in the morning, drinking coffee, and seeing what the new day brings. Every other day meant another long run, and now I didn't have to wait for the weekend to do it. My running times started dropping quite a bit, from very, very slow to just slow. Maybe even average for my age group.

A few months after I left work, we travelled to Dallas to help Rik move out of his house. He was a year out from getting a divorce. We didn't realize how much emotional toll the divorce had taken on him, but when we got to Dallas and saw what a mess his house was, we knew. I took one look at his place and announced I was going back to the hotel to watch the Indians playoff game (it was October). Elaine, of course, being the mom that she is, started helping clean the place out. A week later—somehow—we had him moving into a new apartment. I came up with the idea of cleaning out one room at a time, and I volunteered to run all the books that he needed to get rid of (most of them) to Half Price Books. That was a great week for all the Half Price Books stores within a fifty-mile radius of Dallas. And my "one-room-at-a-time" plan seemed brilliant, almost Einstein-like, to Rik.

It was during that week, with some help from Rik, that I discovered White Rock Lake Park in Dallas. I had to drive from our hotel quite a ways down Mockingbird Lane to get there but it was well worth the trip. What an amazing city park. Firstly, you can actually find plenty of places to park your car. Secondly, it's 9.3 miles around the lake and easy to pull off without getting lost, as long as you stay left at every fork on the pathway. Several mansions and even a few marinas surround the lake itself. And it's the perfect mix of mostly flat with a few steep hills thrown in on the second half of the run. You couldn't design a better nine-mile running path if you were starting from scratch.

It was at White Rock that I started to learn that I was—believe it or not—getting faster. I was averaging just a little over nine-and-a-half-minute miles around the lake: not great but definitely an improvement. Everything is relative for the aging runner. Plus, the runs got me out of helping Rik move for a few hours at time.

We returned to Dallas a month later for Thanksgiving and I signed up for a half marathon around Bachman Lake on the following Saturday. I could tell I was getting in better shape, plus when else was I going to add Texas to my list of states where I had done at least a half? Bachman Lake turned out to be the essence of a more urban city park, much less upscale than White Rock. The morning of the half marathon we headed for the Starbucks I had scouted out near our hotel, as I knew it would be open early enough for me to get coffee before the run. Some things are just a priority; no half marathon is happening for me without coffee first. The guy at Starbucks asked me where I was running that day and when I told him Bachman Lake, he informed me it was a popular place for drug deals. Hmm. Did he have to say that when Elaine was right next to me and right before she was going to be hanging around the lake while I ran?

The morning was chilly, in the low forties and dark at the start. And Bachman Lake was almost as scary as the Starbucks guy had said. I glanced around for drug dealers when we arrived, but no one was holding up a sign saying they were dealing drugs so that was good enough for me.

Elaine and I both like small-time races and this was certainly one. There were no more than two hundred people attending. Some crazy race organizers were actually doing the same race three days in a row at Bachman Lake, with Thanksgiving itself being the first day and this being the third. We started out with a long bible reading while I stood and froze at the starting line, this being Texas and all. Then someone played a scratchy recording of the national anthem. Speaking of patriotism, there was some dude who ran the entire half marathon holding the American flag.

I started out running a decent pace but not too fast. The race course involved running about a half mile out and back, and then running three times around Bachman Lake. This meant that I could pass by Elaine three times during the race and wave to her—as she was gallantly waiting in the cold for me to finish the thing.

Being chilly at the start is always a good sign, as it means that when you warm up you probably won't be too hot. Stunningly, I kept getting faster each lap around the lake. I was running somewhere around 9:45-per-mile pace.

There was a tall thin lady in her forties who kept trading places with me. We passed each other three or four times during the race. Finally, on the last lap around the lake, at about mile eleven, I make a quick move past her and said something encouraging and normal like, "You are doing great," and she replied, "You are looking great." Even in my depleted state, I registered that she meant "not bad for a sixty-year-old guy." I passed her with the conviction that I was not going to let her pass me again. And she didn't. I was trying to break two hours and ten minutes, and I actually finished in two hours, seven minutes, and some seconds. I crossed this finish line proudly and feeling strong—although not exactly like I wanted to run any farther. Wow, maybe I can get faster as I get older.

Shortly before I stopped working, we bought a small condo down in Hilton Head, South Carolina. The logic was foolproof—who can argue with trying to get away from the winters after you have spent a bunch of years in Ann Arbor and Milwaukee? Feeding off the momentum of my Bachman Lake performance, I decided to add a few more states to my "at least a half marathon" list in 2017. This became easier to accomplish when I could use Hilton Head as a launching pad.

I started out by keeping it simple and going for a South Carolina half marathon. Hilton Head had one in February but I wasn't going to be there then, so I ran one in a development called Palmetto Bluff, near Bluffton and across the bridge from Hilton Head. The early-March run was unseasonably cold; I was just as cold at the start as I was back in Dallas. To make sure I had sufficient obstacles, Palmetto Bluff added twenty-five-mile-per-hour winds to the mix.

I started out fast but then crashed (again), ending up running two hours and eleven minutes. And feeling not so great for days afterwards. That's the thing about crashing. The recovery is much worse than if you start slow and run a smart race. In other words, the dumber you are, the more it hurts.

Undaunted and still fired up about having run 2:07-something back in Dallas, I spent the rest of the spring and summer trying to improve my speed. I signed up for an early-October half at Kings Island, an amusement park twenty miles from my house in Cincinnati. The race was advertised as "twice around the amusement park," which turned out to mean two and a half miles in the parking lot (how scenic!), then nearly four miles in the amusement park, then repeat. I lucked out again and the weather at the start was in the forties. I went out way too fast but managed to hang on at the end, and beat my Bachman Lake time by about a minute. It was nice to run a relatively fast time but I did it the hard, painful way.

I decided to run Savannah and knock off Georgia next. The Savannah Rock 'n' Roll Marathon is held the first Saturday in November. I figured it wouldn't be too hot. But on race day it became clear that I had figured wrong. We took off to the north and ran quite a ways through a semi-industrial area. Then, when we turned back to the east, the blazing sun was right in our faces. Even my sunglasses didn't seem to do the trick. Around mile six I realized I couldn't hold my pace, and by mile eight I was struggling. Soon after that came the major, big-league crash. By the last few miles I was alternating between walking and a slow shuffle. The low point, other than the crash, was when I almost spit on two women coming into the finishing chute. I was just too wiped out to be aware of who or what was around me. It could have been a great half, since the crowds were enormous and Savannah is an awesome city, but it just wasn't my day. Instead, I chalked up another one in the "went out too fast" category. To add insult to injury, after the finish I had to walk a good mile to meet Elaine in the hotel lobby.

When I was in high school I played golf, which can be a humbling sport. A very humbling sport. But nothing is more humbling than crashing in a long-distance race. And, as I demonstrated in Savannah, I am still fully capable of that.

10

RUNNING AND ME, ME AND RUNNING

"There is no such thing on earth as an uninteresting subject; the only thing that can exist is an uninterested person."
G.K. Chesterton, Heretics

As I was working on this book, Desiree "Des" Linden won the women's Boston Marathon in April 2018. Nobody expected her to win, because while she is an elite runner, her times are slower than the fastest women marathoners out there. But the weather was terrible, a mix of torrential rain and strong headwinds, all of which she overcame to win. She ran the slowest time of any women's winner in Boston for at least twenty years: two hours, thirty-nine minutes, and fifty-four seconds. About halfway through the race, Des told Shalane Flanagan that she would probably drop out and offered to help her get back to the lead pack before doing so. She then purposefully slowed down to help Shalane. But in the second half of the marathon Des found that she felt better and she started passing other runners. She ended up finishing about five minutes ahead of the second-place finisher. During the post-race interviews, she was a model of humility and class. Marathoning tends to be humbling for even world-class runners.

Des was an unlikely winner, especially since she had to come all the way back from a stress fracture in her hip that caused her to drop out of the 2012 Olympic Marathon in London. But the second-place finisher was even less likely. A nurse anesthesiologist who lives in Tucson, Arizona, Sarah Sellers was a cross-country runner in college but not one with a distinguished running career. Like Des, she had to overcome an injury that prevented her from training for more than a year. She entered Boston, her second marathon ever, mostly because her brother was also running. She spent most of the race tucked into a pack of runners to help break the wind. Then she started passing world-class runners whom she had only read about before the race. She had no idea she was in second place when she finished in two hours and forty-four minutes.

Watching the video replays—and the combination of resilience and humility coming from Des and Sarah in their post-race interviews—still brings tears to my eyes long after the race. Maybe this explains why I keep running, and why I have kept running for over forty years. When I watch them, I realize how totally alive and in-the-moment they were in Boston. Not thinking of the future or the past, but simply putting down their best race. Doing the best that they could possibly do in the moment. All great runs have at least that one thing in common: the runner focuses on nothing but the present moment—the next step, the next hill, the next person in front of you, the next telephone pole, the next water stop. Running is an elegantly simple endeavor. You need to think, but not think too much.

Running also teaches you to deal with adversity. Much of what happens to us in life is not of our choosing. It's a myth to think otherwise. Even the luckiest among us encounter unplanned events where something important has gone horribly wrong. When we think others lead charmed lives, this is mostly because we don't know much about them. Both Des and Sarah went through injuries so challenging they were unsure if they would be able to run again. There have been many times when I have had issues in my life—of all kinds —and the only coherent "plan" that I could come up with in the moment was to go for a run. And, when I did, I felt more alive. This was worth something. I haven't yet mastered the path to enlightenment, but surely it begins with being alive and awake.

In a minimalist sense, running has reminded me that I am still alive and moving forward. I started out running because it would help me feel better on the outside—about my body, my weight, my appearance. I've kept running because it makes me feel better on the inside.

Not everything that we try in life will make sense in the moment that we do it. Steve Jobs, the founder of Apple, gave a famous commencement speech at Stanford shortly after he was first diagnosed with pancreatic cancer. It is a short but wonderful speech, which is often quoted. Among the several wise observations he made was "you can't connect the dots looking forward; you can only connect them looking backward." The flipside of that insight might be that sometimes you shouldn't be too analytical about your decisions before you make them. Much of the learning in life comes from the doing; and in some of the doing we get in deep over our heads.

As I have done in about half of the marathons that I ran.

There are many philosophies of life, many possible ways to look at the world. But in the most rudimentary form, the one that makes the most sense to me is simply to keep going—to get back up every time life knocks you down—and to stay interested; see the possibilities of the world. The essential thing to learn in life is that you are more resilient than you ever thought. Every time I go out for a run it becomes easier for me to believe this about myself.

There are some people who just stop learning and stop growing, which is like stopping living. Anyone who tries to do anything of consequence in this world will be criticized for it; there will be successes and failures, and some perceived successes will actually be the result of treating people poorly. On the other hand, some perceived failures will be rich and meaningful personal experiences for everyone involved. Ultimately, none of this is within our control. But what we can control is whether or not we stay interested in the world. We can make the effort to get back up when life knocks us down. And if you keep getting back up and stay interested, anything is possible. There are always more hills to climb, and your reward for getting over the last one will be the chance to climb another.

I've always been attracted to solving, or at least trying to solve, big problems. Indeed, this became something of a curse in my career because I had a nasty habit of taking on impossible tasks. But it's taken me the better part of a lifetime to realize that *how* you live your life is just as important as *why* you live your life. Dr. George Sheehan was a prominent writer about running from the 1970s to the early 1990s, with regular columns in that early bible of the running movement, *Runner's World*. He once wrote, "If you are seeking solutions for the Great Whys of your creation, you will have to start with the Little Hows of your day-to-day living. If you are looking for answers to the Big Questions about your soul, you'd best begin with the Little Answers about your body."

The most important decision that I ever made about running was simply this: I was going to run as much as I could and as far as I could and as fast as I could for as long as I could, without thinking about it too much. It turns out that if you decide every day whether or not you feel like running, it's much like the writer who decides every day whether or not he or she wants to write. There will be too many days when you don't run, and you will miss the gifts of those days when it was, in fact, the run that could have resurrected the day. It is better to make the decision to be a runner once, and avoid thinking too much until you are at least into mile three . . . or mile six, as the case may be.

Our society and culture are always suggesting that we add things to our lives to make them happier and more meaningful. Every day we are hammered with messaging suggesting that we need more things. If we have one house, we need a bigger one. If we have the bigger one, we need a second vacation home. If we go see a financial advisor, they will always plant a seed of doubt about whether or not we have enough money—no matter how much we have. Our career needs to be better, we need to work harder, we need to get that next promotion.

The world values status and reputation, even though both status and reputation are less important than character. Reputation is who people think we are, but character is who we really are. If you think they are the same, you haven't been paying attention. The world is full of hypocritical behavior. Character is about what we do when no one else is watching.

We're supposed to "network" more, to use social media to build our contacts. We're supposed to figure out how to raise great kids and make a good living at the same time. We're supposed to look presentable all the time, and if we don't there is always someone trying to sell us something to help (especially if we are female). If we are "middle-aged," broadly defined, we are supposed to pay attention to our kids and our spouse and our aging parents all at the same time, and not drop any balls. Oh, and by the way, we're supposed to figure out what to do about our dysfunctional political system and eroding middle class while we are at it. And if all of that pressure to do more makes us feel worse, just hang a minute, the next commercial is about a drug that will make us feel better.

But here's the thing. The world is full of problems and perhaps always will be, as long as flawed human beings inhabit the planet. The thing we need to work on is how to decide when "enough is enough." A friend of mine who advises wealthy people on career issues once said to me, "I can tell you exactly how much money people need—a bit more than what they already have." We don't seem to have that gene that tells us when enough is enough.

Running, for me, has been the great equalizer. It's taught me that less can be more. And it has taught me this not just conceptually and intellectually, but deep in my bones. Sometimes the way to wholeness is to let go and subtract things from your life, rather than just trying to cram more in. Running has brought me back to the basics, back to the present moment when I don't know how else to get there.

When we can find our self in the present moment—when we can

learn again how to breathe and feel and see the world with the eyes of the beginner—that's when we become more human. And that's when we can give to others and to the world, expecting nothing in return.

EPILOGUE

"All dreams are crazy. Until they come true."
Nike Ad

IT IS CHRISTMASTIME 2017. Elaine and Rik and I decide to spend a few days in Greenville, South Carolina—Elaine and I stay overnight there often, splitting up our drive between Cincinnati and Hilton Head. I want to show Rik what amazing things a small city can do with a downtown and a river.

It's a midweek morning and colder than I'd like. The snow swirls through the cloudy skies but is not sticking to the ground. I lace up my running shoes, put on the running shorts that I always wear no matter the weather, and throw on my stocking cap and gloves. I pass over my heavy gray hooded sweatshirt, fearing it will bog down my run. Instead, I opt for my new, lighter blue running jacket even though I know I will start out freezing. I pour some Gatorade into my water bottle and take off in a brisk walk from the Marriott down towards the Reedy River.

Five minutes later I cross the pedestrian bridge over the river and onto the Swamp Rabbit Trail, which runs along the river bank for thirty miles or so northeast of town. It's my kind of trail—mostly for bikers and paved the whole way, no dirt, with half-mile markers that actually sync up with my watch. I am right about freezing. I hit that now-or-never moment where you either need to start running or walk back to the hotel and fetch something warmer to wear. I always just start running. The cold wind hits my face as I take off, making the caffeine from my morning Starbucks irrelevant. I am nothing if not awake.

For the first mile I am cursed by my monkey mind. I cannot think straight about anything other than how I cold I am, how much my muscles hurt, and how much I wish the wind would stop. I feel like the sixty-year-old guy that I am. I pass five people walking or running the other way back into town. We nod to each other, tacitly acknowledging our mutual craziness society. There is no need to say it out loud. I stop to cross the two busy streets that come up abruptly, with drivers who seem unaware of the Swamp Rabbit Trail and the significance of my morning run. It's clear that it's my job to look out for them. I cross by the train tracks that have four or five posted warning signs, although I've never seen an actual train.

The trail is slick but not icy. It turns out even beautiful running trails don't attract lots of runners on 30-degree days in the Southeast. I pass the marker that tells me I am only a half mile from the famous Swamp Rabbit Cafe. To some the Cafe is a bike shop, to others a health food store, to many a hip coffee shop. To me it is a restroom stop with some lemonade-like health drink that is close enough to Gatorade. The Cafe always shows up at the perfect time. I pass by the counter, saying hello to the carryout clerk as if I am on a shopping spree, and make a mad dash to the restroom. I have this maneuver down pat. Always say hello and act like you are going to take home three grocery bags. The clerk is likely onto the gig but goes along with it, which I appreciate.

I take off from the Cafe down the winding trail, over the pedestrian bridges, and up towards the Appalachian foothills, up towards the rest of my life. I don't have a plan, but the wind is in my face and the trail is trending upward, which is exactly what I want. I run for two more miles before I realize that I have not seen a soul—no runners, no bikers, no walkers. I am no longer cold. It is just me and my breath and the occasional squirrel scampering out of the deepening woods. I am running with ease, heel to toe, heel to toe, over and over again. I've never seen myself run, but Elaine—who is hardly unbiased—says that I look like a natural. No bounce, no need to speed up or slow down. I have no need to see anyone, to talk to anyone.

My heart, perhaps even my soul and spirit, tells me that I can keep running like this forever, all the way to where I am going, wherever that is. My mind knows better, but right now my heart is winning out. My body is quiet, complaining about nothing. Every once in a while, my right foot aches a little, reminding me how the young doctor told me ten years ago with a youthful grin, "Oh, that's just arthritis that you get when you get older." What a dickhead. But even that foot is mostly quiet now too, like it wants in to the dance. I'm in that place, that zone, where I believe that everything will work out if I just keep putting one foot in front of the other. I know I am deluding myself but I don't care about that.

I come across a sign that says it's a mile to Furman University. The trail juts uphill steeply to the left. I think about my sister, Robin. Not a religious man, running like this is where I mostly feel her presence. I think about Rik. Not being his father but not exactly being not-his-father either, I feel proud. I think about Elaine, who is always there, always smiling, always asking about how my run went, when I get back. The only time I ever told her not to worry before I went out, you'll recall I tripped over the sidewalk twelve miles into my thirteen-miler, fell on my face, broke my glasses, and ended up in the emergency room getting stitches. So, I don't say that anymore.

Eventually, I get too tired to think much at all. It is now just about putting one foot in front of the other. I hit Furman University and come across a beautiful lake. There might be a sign warning that you are supposed to have a campus ID or something ridiculous. I ignore it. I stop my watch and walk slowly around the lake. I ignore the young couples with kids; I ignore the runners who might be forty years younger than me; I ignore the world outside my run.

The sun is peeking through the clouds, showing up a few hours late. I don't hold it against the sun; I am glad to be warmer. I hit the watch again and begin a gentle jog downhill, back to Greenville, back to my life. A sometimes-anxious man, I am calm. An analytical man by any account, I am thinking about nothing but the next step. A goal-oriented man, I have no goals. What will be, will be. My body moves seamlessly, gracefully, and without much effort. Each part entirely in sync with the whole. I might even be Dave Wottle in those last 100 meters in Munich 1972, except that I know that I am not.

There is much to sort out in this world. It can be a complicated place. Mostly, with a little help from your friends, you need to sort it out for yourself. Only you can find your trail. No one else can tell you how to live your life, or should.

But, on that cold December morning in Greenville, I'm not thinking about any of that. In fact, I'm not thinking at all. I simply feel wonder.

I am, at long last, in the world but not of it.

The ground feels soft below my feet. I will be back soon enough.

ACKNOWLEDGMENTS

This is the hardest page of the book to write. How do you figure out who to thank in a lifetime filled with kind and caring people? Here goes anyway.

I'd like to thank the family I grew up in—my parents, Bob and Sue, my sisters, Susan and Robin, and my brother Scott—without whom there would literally be no book to write, and certainly not this one.

Thank you to all of the wonderfully talented and deeply caring people that I worked with over many years, who always gave me a reason to come to work.

Thank you to my friends from where I grew up, Bowling Green, for one of the best childhoods anyone could imagine and for being lifelong friends.

Thanks to Clark Richardson, Chris Nerney, and Alan Ying, for always being there —even when the chips were down.

Thanks to Rachael Herron for your support and guidance, always delivered with great humor. Thank you to Bryony Sutherland, a very talented editor with a dazzling combination of edge and empathy.

All of the flaws in this book, as well as all of the flaws in my life, are my responsibility. But however flawed, my life is made immeasurably better by my uniquely wonderful wife Elaine—who supports me unconditionally, irrespective of the facts at hand. Everyone would be lucky to have someone like her in their corner, but I am the only one quite that lucky—since there is only one of her. And I am immensely proud of my stepson Rik Adamski, who accepts me as I am and does not make fun of my age, except when we talk about music.

ABOUT THE AUTHOR

Doug Schneider is a runner, writer, and university lecturer on the changing workplace. He spent over twenty years in the healthcare information technology industry, leading and working on talented teams that drove industry expansion and innovation. He resides in Cincinnati, Ohio and Hilton Head, South Carolina with his wife Elaine.

Doug's writing on life, work, and running can be found at www.dougschneider.net and he can also be reached by email at marathon-doug@hotmail.com.

RECOMMENDED READING

Run Forever, Your Complete Guide to Healthy Lifetime Running by Amby Burfoot

Once a Runner by John L Parker

Self Aware: A Guide to Success in Work and Life by Robert Pasick and Dunrie Greiling

Fast-Draft Your Memoir: Write Your Life Story in 45 Hours by Rachael Herron

The Five Secrets You Must Discover Before You Die by John Izzo

Thank you for reading !! If you enjoyed this book, please consider posting a review. Even if it's only a few sentences, it would be a huge help.

Made in the USA
Columbia, SC
26 April 2020